Gunfighting, and Other Thoughts about Doing Violence, Volume One Rev. 0.4

©*2012 by CR Williams and In Shadow In Light*

Table of Contents

TO THE READER..6

WHAT CAN YOU DO <u>NOW</u>?...............................8

About The Pictures In This Book.........................10

About The Content Of This Book.........................13

PART ONE:
MENTAL, MORAL, PHYSICAL

WHY DOES IT VEX SOME PEOPLE THAT HAN SOLO (MAY HAVE) FIRED FIRST?............................16

TRAINING YOUR MIND TO FIGHT............................19

SHOOTING AND FIGHTING: THERE IS A DIFFERENCE..24

THE COUNTERATTACKING MIND............................29

YES, YOU CAN BUY SKILL...................................38

PATTRNING CHAOS...44

WHAT DO YOU KNOW?..49

LABELS..55

BEING LIKE JOHN WAYNE CAN'T BE ALL BAD.......59

GETTING TO GRIPS WITH A DIFFERENT HAMMER..63

IN CONSIDERATION OF THE ACTIVE SHOOTER..................69

PELVIC SHOTS AND BEING 'BATMAN WITH A GUN'..................72

CAN YOU SHOOT SOMEBODY YOU *KNOW*?..................77

YOU *WILL* HAVE BAD DAYS AT THE RANGE..................79

PART TWO:
THE ART, THE SCIENCE, THE METHOD

WE USUALLY DO THIS BACKWARDS, DON'T WE?..................84

RANGE SAFETY, COMBAT SAFETY..................85

THE DRAWSTROKE..................86

A NEED FOR SPEED?..................96

THERE IS NO CONTROVERSY..................103

WHAT THEY'RE NOT TELLING YOU ABOUT POINT SHOOTING..................109

ANOTHER DEFINITION OF POINT SHOOTING..................116

ACCURACY IS KING (BUT MONARCHS DO FALL)..122

CARRYING WITHOUT A ROUND CHAMBERED..123

RESISTING A HOME INVASION I: IMMEDIATE ACTION DRILLS..126

RESISTING A HOME INVASION II: TOOLS, TACTICS, TECHNIQUES..134

RIGHT HAND, LEFT HAND, ONE HAND, BOTH HANDS, EITHER HAND..142

NICE DRAWSTROKE: CAN YOU DO THAT ONE-HANDED?..156

THE FLOATING GUN..164

CONSISTENCY, THE CONCEPT..170

THERE'S ONLY ONE WAY..176

PORTING A CARRY GUN IS A BAD IDEA..................................180

SELF-DEFENSE WITH THE LONG GUN..................................184

HERE BEGINNETH THE LESSON.........186

RESOURCES..194

ABOUT THE AUTHOR..200

GRATITUDE..201

Why I'm Calling This "Revision 0.6"

Some material has been modified or edited to allow for changes to people and things referenced, to changes in information about something or better information about something, to update any techniques that now have better replacements and to correct errors of various kinds, mostly small ones of editing and the like. I have also replaced a number of the photos used here with what I hope are better ones. The biggest change is in the size of the printed book. To make it a bit more convenient to you to carry, I have moved to a smaller size. There have been no large-scale changes, so am borrowing from software update practice and calling this an incremental, not a full-version, update.

TO THE READER

The content of this book confines itself almost completely to contemplation of lethal-force attacks—attacks meant to kill, maim, or cause grave injury or harm. This book does not consider anything other than lethal-force attacks that require lethal-force responses. This should not be taken as advising the reader about responses to less than lethal-force felony assault. Neither should anything in this book be taken as legal or technical guidance to you, the reader. This content of this book is intended for information and consideration, to provoke thought and discussion, and to encourage those who read it to seek professional advice and instruction. That is the primary and central intent of this book. Consult with local authorities and those knowledgeable of the laws regarding and restricting use of force at all levels in their area, and to educate themselves so that they can, ahead of time, know how best to respond to assault. Do not wait to be attacked to think about what the law says you can or can't do, and don't wait until you are attacked to develop the skills you need to survive the attack.

Do your homework now, do your thinking about legal response and force levels before and not during the attack, and get the training that will help you avoid an attack or survive one sooner rather than later.

No one involved in the production or publication of this book assumes responsibility or liability for any accident or injury that readers may put upon themselves by any use or misuse, interpretation or misinterpretation of this material. **This book is not a substitute for guidance and training by a professional instructor. What you do with the information and opinions contained herein and the results and the consequences of any action you take is your responsibility and yours <u>only</u>.**

By continuing on with the reading of this book, you acknowledge that you understand your full and complete responsibility for your own safety, accept that responsibility, and agree that all parties involved with production, publication, and distribution of this book and supporting media and materials will not be held responsible in <u>any way</u> for <u>anything</u> that may happen because of use or misuse of any information contained herein.

Thank you, and good luck as you begin and/or continue your training and education.

INTRODUCTION: WHAT CAN YOU DO NOW?

There really are people that have an actual need to not have their names made public, and there are real reasons why they have that need. One of those people is a Suarez International Specialist Instructor that posts on the Warrior Talk Internet forum under the user-name of "Cold War Scout."

He has a lot of interesting and useful things to say, CWS does, and a lot of useful and interesting questions to ask us. One of the questions of particular interest to me right now, as well as being the point of this introduction, went something like this:

What you could do twenty years ago, or even ten years ago, might be interesting but does it really matter NOW? No. What you could do 'back in the day' doesn't matter. What matters is what you can do RIGHT HERE, RIGHT NOW. The trouble that you handled a decade back in the 'good old days' isn't the trouble that's coming to you now. WHAT CAN YOU DO NOW? Are you ready to throw down RIGHT HERE AND RIGHT NOW if you need to, if you have to? ARE YOU? CAN YOU?

I was once a Suarez International Staff Instructor, and I could answer that question in one way: I can teach. I can be an instructor. Then I was what the military calls a 'heat casualty', and because of that, I can't 'throw down' as an instructor for now, and am currently a Retired Suarez International Staff Instructor. But Cold War Scout's question still has to be answered. What can I do NOW?

The book you are reading is one of the answers to that question. Because I cannot currently run a class like I used to, but I can still teach. I cannot currently lead students up to the firing line, but I can still point them at useful knowledge. I cannot currently step up and directly correct a student one-on-one, but I can get some people to correct themselves by asking the right questions and provoking them to answer.

I can help them begin to answer the 'CWS question', correctly.

That's what I can do now.

What can you do?

Hopefully, something here will help you answer that question the right way, some day, when life is on the line.

Good luck.

ABOUT THE PICTURES IN THIS BOOK

All the safety rules were followed in the production of the photographs used in this book. In all cases where shooting was not involved, verified-empty weapons or replica weapons were used. Where a weapon is pointed at the camera, it is either a replica, empty, or the camera is unattended. Where live-fire is shown, either the photographer is behind the line of fire or the camera is being operated on a timer or remotely. No one was allowed to 'break the plane' at any point of a live-fire sequence.

In pictures where I am illustrating working from concealment I will be dressed as you see me here. This is the way I often dress outside of work--an untucked shirt, usually a t-shirt (which you will see in other pictures), inexpensive but serviceable pants, and, usually,

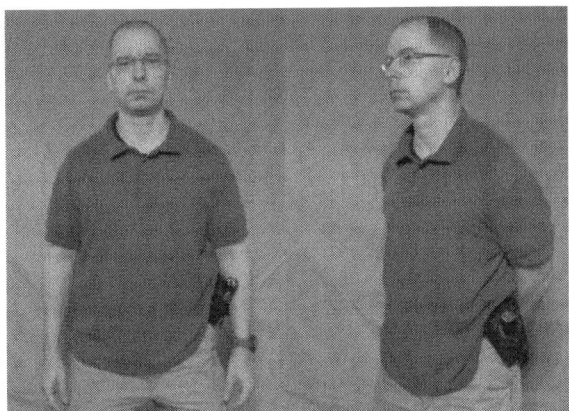

boots. The Maxpedition pouch is, as you see it here, is generally left outside of cover so as to make it less likely that someone thinks it's the gun and calls in a report, besides providing a modest misdirection from where the gun really is. It carries my phone, a flashlight, two pens, and a mechanical pencil. (I will soon swap phones and move to separate carriers for the phone by itself and the flashlight. The pens and mini-screwdriver [I keep that at hand as part of my job of being a professional geek.] will likely be split between those two carriers. I will still keep them in the open like this.)

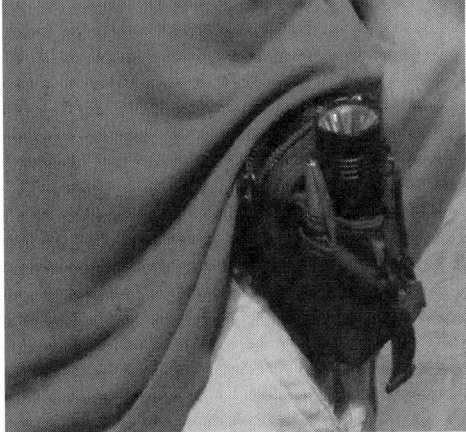

This is normal dress for me and a lot of other people, not the photographer's or fishing vests (or 'tactical' vests) I often see worn in videos or photos in books and magazines with a pistol carried in the open. That's not real to me. This is. I want you to see how it works when the instructor is not 'dressed for success' as they often are for such videos and photo shoots. It's not as neat-looking as what they wear, I'll grant you. But neither is life outside of the range or the photo shoot, and neither is the gunfight.

So if all you want are some pretty pictures, you may have to get another book. But if you want as much honesty about the fight and the realities of it as I can provide you, whether my shirt is tucked in or not, then stay with me and I'll do what I can not to disappoint you about that.

My thanks to the Central Alabama Gun Club for allowing me to use their excellent facility for some of the photographs used in this book.

A NOTE ABOUT THE CONTENT OF THIS BOOK

Most of the material in this first volume of what I intend to be a series of books has been collected from one of four sources: Articles written for Concealed Carry Magazine, a publication produced by the United States Concealed Carry Association; articles written for a weekly newsletter that USCCA produces and publishes on the Internet; articles written for Warrior Talk News, a blog and newsletter produced and published by Suarez International; and from postings on various Internet forums where I have been or currently am active. There is some expansion of previously-published material and some material not previously published anywhere else, but with few exceptions, most of this has been collected and collated from the afore-mentioned sources. Pictures have been added to help expand on some concepts, and things organized to follow and complement each other to create a whole that I believe will be much more useful to you than if you went through (assuming you could find everything) all of the material separately as it was originally published.

In addition, material expanding on and/or related to the work here will be placed on my company website on an ongoing basis. Such additional work will continue as subsequent volumes are published.

Finally, a legal note. I retain all required rights and/or have permission to publish all material and supporting material included here.

All that concluded, I think it is past time to get to the good stuff. Don't you?

PART ONE: MENTAL, MORAL, PHYSICAL

WHY DOES IT VEX SOME PEOPLE THAT HAN SOLO (MAY HAVE) FIRED FIRST?

Many of you will recall the scene as it was first done on the first version of the first Star Wars movie. You know, the one that wasn't really the first, unless you're one of those people that doesn't acknowledge the first three as the first three. But I digress.

Luke and Obi-Wan hit the bar looking for a ship, they find Solo, who has a ship, they make a deal and leave, Green Guy (I don't want to worry about remembering his name, so I'll just call him Green Guy.) comes in and sits down with the gun in his hand. There's a conversation that ends with Green Guy declaring how happy he is about being able to kill Han and a response and then a couple of shots, one from each gun, <u>very</u> closely spaced in time.

There was (maybe still is) enough debate about who shot first in the original scene that even someone like me, who is more annoyed by this intrusion on their consciousness than interested in it, became conscious of it. And apparently there were enough people vexed by the question, or vexed by the idea that Han shot first, that Lucas made a point of re-dubbing that scene in subsequent versions of the movie. Or maybe Lucas was vexed by the impression that Han shot first and changed it on his own. Either way, somebody got vexed about it and the scene was modified.

    Here is my proposition: If you carry a gun with the idea that it may be necessary to use it to fight another person in defense of life one day, <u>you should be okay and in agreement with the idea that Solo deliberately set up and took the first shot</u>.*

    The reasons why you should be okay with that are what this part of the book is about.

    If you're going to carry a weapon, a firearm specifically, at all and especially regularly--or even if you're only keeping one at a particular place for defense--I think that preparing mentally, 'setting' your mind up ahead of time, is THE most important thing you can do, and what you should do if you want to survive that fight for existence that may never come, as well as the aftermath of that fight that may never come. That's why this part of the book is first, and why I consider it to be more important to read through and consider this part than any of the rest of what I write here, for all that I write more about other things than this. Because if the mind is not right before-hand, all else will be threatened, all else will be lessened, and all else may be rendered useless to you and others you care about in the very moment when everything is threatened and when everything is demanded of you if you are to go through it all the way to the end and to your survival and victory.

    I also recognize that you may read and consider what follows as carefully and fully as I wish you to and still <u>not</u> agree with what I propose. It may even vex you as much as it vexes some that Han seems to have fired first. Honestly speaking, I won't like your disagreement and I won't like your vexation if that's what you feel after reading it. I will accept it, though, and I will thank you then as I thank you now if you have considered what I say here and not rejected it without consideration. You have, agreeing or not, given me a fair hearing, and that's all I ask of you and as much as I can expect from anyone, is it not?

Proceed, then, and see why I think that Han Solo was right to do what I think he did, and why I think it would be right for you to do the same thing if you were in the same circumstances that he was in that movie.

*If you're interested in my specific reasoning, here it is: Someone that had just told him flat out that he was going to kill him had a gun on him. Green Guy had Motive, Means, and Opportunity; that's the legal trifecta and justification for Solo to do the covert draw and shoot under the table. He would not, even today (except perhaps in a few jurisdictions) be required to show the gun or warn Green Guy before he fired. Even in jurisdictions that still require retreat before defense, this is justifiable because everybody knows you can't outrun a gun (or blaster) shot.

TRAINING YOUR MIND TO FIGHT

It may be expressed as LEAVE ME ALONE. It may be expressed as DON'T HURT ME. It may be expressed as HOW DARE YOU. It may be expressed as I WANT TO GO HOME. It may be expressed as NOT THIS TIME or NEVER AGAIN. It may not be expressed by anything but action—a silent scream of indignant rage as Good advances to fight Evil. It may be driven by fear or anger or both at the same time. It may be considered, or it may be automatic.

What 'it' is, is the mindset of anyone who has been attacked and forced to counter-attack to survive. It is the attitude taken on the instant of realization that it really is 'FIGHT OR DIE'. It is the ultimate in task-orientation and fixation with one goal: WIN.

(Why WIN and not SURVIVE? Because if you don't win, you probably won't survive. Simple as that.)

So WINNING is what this part of the book is about.

As change is a fact of life, so change is a fact of the world of the civilian defender, those of us preparing against the possibility of violence coming upon us or to someone near to us without warning. Stand up, lock in, get the sights on is changing to get moving, there are other ways to aim, get the hits on. Double-tap and assess has been exchanged for shoot until they stop or shoot until they fall. Revolvers are being exchanged for semiautomatics, shooting with one hand as needed is being taught again, and the strict line between sighted and point shooting is crumbling like the Berlin Wall did over twenty years ago.

This part of the book represents another change, one that acknowledges this real-world necessity: **We cannot defend without attacking**. There are two reasons for this. One, the weapons we use to defend ourselves with are offensive weapons, not shields and barriers. They do not stop force, they project it. That is <u>offensive</u>. That is <u>attacking</u>. What is different, then, about our use of these weapons? We only use them to counter an attack upon us. As someone attacks us, we <u>counter</u>-attack to stop them from killing us. We do not start the attack, we respond to the attack, but we do it by attacking the attacker back. We do this justifiably, with the law on our side, and we are able to articulate our need to counter-attack to anyone who needs or wants to understand what we did.

The second reason we cannot defend without attacking is that we cannot perfectly and purely defend against everything and anyone that attacks us. Every pure defense will fail, and when that defense fails, we will die. Others may die with us. Or perhaps worse, we will see others die without being able to defend them even if we can perfectly defend ourselves.

So we must respond to aggression with aggression. We must, to paraphrase George Washington, be prepared to fight at any time if we are to be at peace. Not only that, but we must be prepared to fight, to move aggressively, to counter-attack with little or no warning.

How do we do that?

Mind-Set. We Set our Minds up ahead of time so that the stimulus (the violent attack against us) triggers the response (the aggressive counter-attack that saves us). We do this first with our conscious minds using methods I will suggest shortly and others that we find effective. The training of our conscious minds will then Set our subconscious minds, and we will forget the Set (In a manner of speaking, that is. We will continue to practice and reinforce the Set just as we continue to practice and reinforce physical skills of defensive offence.) and continue with the business of the day. Most of us will never see the result of that Set because we will never see the thing that triggers it. Those of us that see the triggering action, however—if we have done it right—will show our attackers the real Mind and Spirit of the prepared defender. We will use whatever we have and whatever we can get and we will <u>fight</u>.

Best of all, if we get the Mind Set right, we may not ever have to fight. Once properly integrated, the attitude will come subtlety through where it can be seen by those who look for it. You will not have to be consciously overt about it, and you will not have to make an effort to project it. But it will be there for those that know how to look to see. (How do I know this? I know a few very dangerous men and women, and I know how they look and act. All of them so far that I have known and met were unfailingly friendly and polite and considerate of others. And I would not mess with any one of them for a truckload of gold and the promise of another after I made the mistake of attacking them. They do not project any obvious "don't mess with me, I'm dangerous to mess with" signals, and there is nothing truly overt about their dangerous competence as they go about their business. But it's there. I can feel it.) Those who are predatory who know what to look for—not all do—will see it and know that there will be a cost, a price to pay for attacking you or those close to you. Criminals calculate risk like any business person, and the smart ones will pass you over in search of someone who will not go after them instead of giving up. It's not a perfect defense. What is? But it will help.

So what can you do to develop this Mindset? How can you train yourself to go from peace to War without warning? Here are a few suggestions:

Spend some time with those that you know or believe do have the mindset. Note: It will likely not be obvious and overt; in my experience with the dangerously competent, it is usually not. I have learned, in fact, to suspect those who are too overt and obvious about their fierceness and/or combat competency.

Develop yourself and your skills and abilities. Take classes, train with others, and practice on your own. Becoming confident that you <u>can</u> do makes it easier to set yourself up so that, when necessary, you <u>will</u> do.

As you train your body, train your mind. Focus in training on the attacking defensive attitude. Work through situations and what-ifs in your mind at varying levels and intensity. Run the mental practice up from idle-time-daydream level to full-blown visualizations like athletes and soldiers go through. Over and over again in your mind, see yourself moving immediately to the aggressive defense. See and feel your mind and attitude change instantly as you and others need it to in the moment of crisis. Carry through and see yourself stopping the attacker with efficiency and effectiveness. Knowing that the mind affects the body which affects the mind, practice mental and physical skills in your mind from time to time to supplement and reinforce the physical practice that starts you on the way to setting your mind up for the sudden fight.

As part of your mental training, listen to and read, and then consider, what others have to say about the counter-offensive mindset and how to develop it. As with other things combative, examine every idea, determine what works for you, keep that, and discard the rest.

You do not have to accept everything I or others say, but do please consider it. Whether you accept anything here and act on it or not, begin to develop the single most important part of your 'weapon system'. Begin to develop the mind that moves the hand that fires the gun. Begin to develop the thought that precedes the action.

Begin here. Begin now.

Good luck to us all.

SHOOTING AND FIGHTING: THERE IS A DIFFERENCE

I have a friend who lives up north of me. Young fella. Likes rifles. Has an M14 he's particularly enamored of. Carries a pistol, a Glock of some sort, daily. But you can tell he really doesn't think about it as much as he does the rifles. (This may have changed since I first wrote this as an article and I hope it has, because it's more likely he'll have to use the pistol than the rifle.)

I'll tell you how I know (aside from because of our ongoing discussions about rifles--another essay about that later). About two weeks ago (at the time of this writing), he said this to me in a message:

"Man did you know that I've NEVER practiced drawing from concealment? Nope... not even one practice draw. Pretty crazy, eh?"

Now, I know he practices shooting with the pistol. He's said as much. Maybe not more than I do, but quite a bit nonetheless. I would not be surprised if he was a better shot than I was if it was pure shooting we were talking about.

But since we weren't talking about pure shooting, my response was:

"No, it's not crazy...it's STUPID."

Fortunately, I responded to him before I thought about it, because if I had thought about it before I responded, I would have gotten angry--like I did after I sent the response and did have time to think about it--and if I had been angry when I wrote back, then I would have risked not getting the point across to him properly, that point being...

IT'S NOT ABOUT SHOOTING - IT'S ABOUT FIGHTING.

Understand, please, before we go on... History is full of cases and examples of men and women who did nothing more than obtain a weapon, whether it was a gun or a knife or a pointed stick, set that weapon aside and never pick it up again until the day they used that weapon to successfully fight off an attack. There are, I have no doubt, thousands upon thousands who have not thought of fighting until the very moment when they realized that they had to, and then without training or experience, that's what they did, and successfully. There is no question of that.

A question I do have, however, is how many others who obtained the same kind of weapon and set it aside later died because they did not know how to fight with it. How many more good people would we have, how many less bad people would there be, if only some of them had gone beyond just running a few shots through to test it, or beyond standing and shooting at a target every so often. How many would have lived if they had understood in time that there's a difference between fighting with a gun and shooting a gun?

This is what I wonder about.

And don't get me wrong, either--you need to be able to shoot before you start learning to fight with a pistol...or a rifle or a shotgun, for that matter. When someone is trying to kill you, it is a Good Thing to have the sight picture, master grip, trigger control, and other fundamentals set down as automatically as possible. To have the best chance of winning the fight, you have to go through the basics--how to form a fist, how to set your foot for a kick, how to grip the knife, how to work the trigger on the pistol so you can get the sight picture back after the last shot, things like that. It helps to have a workable grasp of the techniques. You don't need an absolute mastery, just the workable grasp. But you do need them.

And you need to understand that those techniques are not the same thing as fighting.

You can put two shots into a circle the size of a quarter from twenty yards away.

That's shooting. That's not the fight.

Can you put three to five shots into the heart and lungs of a man seven yards away, aiming a gun at you, screaming murder, you shooting one-handed as you run or jump ten feet to where you can get your car's engine block between you and the bullet that he's about to fire at you?

That's not just shooting. That's the fight.

From the holster, you can put the first shot in the A-Zone of an IDPA target twenty feet away in less than 1.25 seconds by the timer.

That's shooting. That's not the fight.

Practicing shooting vs. practicing the shot(s). It may not be easy to see, but many of the same principles apply between the two if you're going to be successful. But unless the difference between the two is understood and applied in training, you stand to lose much more than points on a scorecard or a quarter-inch off a group on a target.

Can you drop your newspaper, draw from under your buttoned suit coat, and start pumping rounds into the person that announced their psychotic break by screaming and pulling a knife as they charge at you from thirty feet away before they get in edge's reach of you? Can you do that even as your body naturally and desperately and automatically tries to put the newsstand or the park bench between you and the screaming psycho? And what if you're sitting on that park bench when the attack starts?

That's not just shooting. That's the fight.

You need to know the difference. You need, like my friend does now, to realize the difference. And like my friend has started doing now, you need to train for the fight and not for the shot.

It could be important.

It could be the difference between living and dying for you.

And if that difference is not important...what is?

THE COUNTERATTACKING MIND

"The purpose of fighting is to win.
There is no possible victory in defense.
The sword is more important than the shield
and skill is more important than either.
**The final weapon is the brain.
All else is supplemental.**"
--John Steinbeck

"Igitur qui desiderat pacem, praeparet bellum."
(Paraphrasing) "If you want to have peace, be prepared to fight for it."

For the civilian defender, here are the dichotomies as I see them:

We live in a peaceful world, but we see a need to be able to enter a violent world at any time with little or no warning.

We provide ourselves with offensive weapons to defend ourselves with.

We plan and prepare to defend ourselves against force by projecting force.

Two of the contradictions we accept if we carry guns: We may have to go from peace to war without any warning, and we defend ourselves and others by projecting force.

We have to. We have no other choice if we do not choose to surrender to whatever violence is offered to us. There is no perfect defense. No shield…No armor…No barrier…Nothing that man has produced will stop every attack, every bit of force offered, every strike and stab and bullet, every time, all the time. "This (device, substance, technique) will stop most attacks that you are likely to be subject to," someone says. Is "most" good enough for you? Let's put a figure on it— 97%. This—whatever—will stop 97% of all attacks. Do you want to risk being in the 3% of cases where it doesn't? And do you want to believe that an attacker, without being resisted, will not continue, will not repeat the attack until they hit the golden 3% mark?

Reality is that most of us already have those odds of not being successfully attacked without the magical armor or miraculous technique, because most of us will not be attacked at all. The odds that you will be attacked some time in your life, however, are lower than the odds of winning almost any lottery you can name, and we know that people win lotteries all the time.

So we're back to the dichotomies. We're back to carrying weapons and learning hand-to-hand combat. We're back to being able to project force to resist force projected at us. We're back to attacking the one who first attacks us.

Defend myself with a gun? How? Do I use it to stop bullets or deflect the blade of the knife thrust at my face? No: I use the gun to stop the *attacker*, not the *attack*. How do I stop the attacker with a gun? I shoot him. I don't take the gun and put it against his arm or hand or trigger finger to block his action. I shoot him with it. I point the gun and I pull the trigger and I project force enough (I hope) that he becomes unable or unwilling to keep projecting force at me. I attack back. I attack the attacker.

I ATTACK.

And so do you. You also attack—or to be more accurate, you and I counter-attack, because we know that will be the only way to stop the attack once it has begun. We acknowledge the reality that Steinbeck speaks of, which is that pure defense, however perfect, does not produce victory (however we define victory at the time).

The reality is that we must have the sword and we must attack back with it. It may not even be a physical sword…we are discussing mindset here, after all…and it may not be a physical attack even if we have a physical sword, or knife, or gun, in our hands, but it will be a counter-<u>attack</u> regardless. It is an attack made in response to an attack (against our body or our mind and spirit or both at once) which is intended to stop the attack against us from continuing.

This is <u>not</u> how you defend yourself with the gun. It's not a shield. You can't and don't use it like one. You don't use it to block or deflect force.

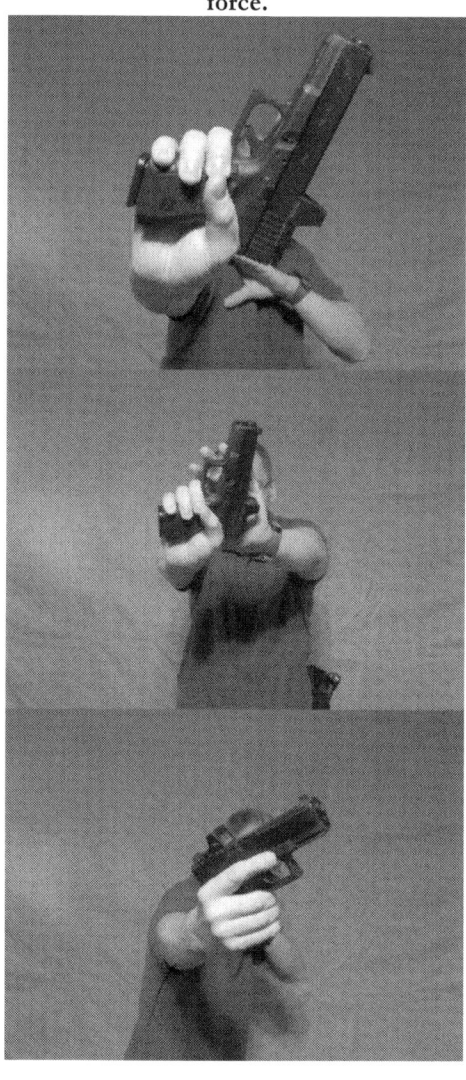

<u>This</u> is how you defend yourself with a gun--by projecting <u>force</u> to counter the force applied against you. (The beginning of movement off the centerline is more purely defensive, but even that is done as much to facilitate the counterattack as to avoid the incoming attack.)

Whether we do that by affecting the will of the attacker alone (and this is the most effective thing we can do to stop them) or by affecting both the will of the attacker and their physical ability to attack (by damaging them) or, worst case, by affecting just their physical ability to attack (and where their will remains, this is the hardest option of the three to accomplish), we must still counter-attack. Whether we use a gun or a knife, pepper spray or bare hands, *we must still counter-attack*. Whether we do that by exploding off the X, dynamically drawing, and running a burst of rounds up their centerline or by standing tall, locking the gun out and the sights on and sending a round precisely into the base of the attacker's nose from sixty feet away, **we must still counter-attack**.

To do otherwise is to risk death. To think of defense alone is to risk death. To think of what others will think of us in that moment, because of what we did, is to risk death. To worry about courts and lawyers when the attack is upon us is to risk death. To think of the sword as a shield is to risk death. Our death, the deaths of others, the death of the way we live that occurs if those who are evil are able to do evil things to us and those we love. To properly defend against that death, physical and not, we must in the moment of the threat put aside thoughts of defense alone. We must take up the sword, and we must attack those who have attacked us, and we must do it until we win, however we define winning at that time and place.

Not only must we counter-attack, but we must do that with all the force and aggressiveness we can muster. We cannot afford to measure the counter-attack until we have, without any doubt, dominated the attacker. We cannot think of a certain number of rounds fired, we cannot think of a certain number of stabs or slashes with the knife, we cannot think of certain blows with the hands and feet. We cannot think of this before, and we cannot think of it during. We must think only of results—getting results, measuring results, observing results, acting upon results. No pre-set limits; only results.

To set limits is to, again, increase the risk of death.

Reality Says: *Think ATTACK, not defense.*

Reality Says: RESULTS MATTER.

Because of that, we must consider Mindset

What is your Mission??

There are missions, and there are Missions. Small 'm' missions come and go and vary in importance depending on time and place and circumstances; large 'M' Missions, are the core, the central theme and focus, that all the small m's support and move you to. There will be many missions, but for each major area of your life, only one Mission. I submit to you that developing the proper mindset for no-notice counter-offense begins and depends on you developing or discovering your Mission.

In the first part of the movie 'Saving Private Ryan', Captain Miller says, as best as I can recall, "If finding this guy gets me home to my wife sooner, then that's my mission." His mission, his immediate goal and task, is to find Private Ryan and get him headed home. His Mission, the ultimate goal and his central task, is to go home to his wife. Everything else he does in the movie is in support of that Mission.

At the end of the movie we see the older Ryan as he falls to his knees at Miller's grave and says to his wife, "Tell me I've been a good man." This is because, when Miller died in the defense of the bridge, his last words to Ryan were "…*earn* this. *Earn it.*" Whatever Ryan's Mission was before that time, I believe that after hearing those words it became, Be A Good Man. Everything else he did after that in his life was in support of that Mission. His question to his wife could have been, "Have I accomplished my Mission? Have I?"

Your Mission does not have to be kept in your conscious mind. Miller was more conscious of his Mission than Ryan was in the movie. While you do, I believe, decide or discover consciously what your Mission is, once you've done that, and once you understand that it is THE Mission and not a waypoint, you can mostly stop thinking about it a lot. Your subconscious mind will understand its importance and maintain the focus on it that you need for decision-making and action after that.

Your Mission should be simple in concept. Other, small 'm', missions can be as complex as they need to be to be understood and accomplished, but the core Mission, the one that drives you forward, past or, if necessary, through any obstacle, should be as simple as it needs to be. The subconscious will do simple better than complex. It will focus easier on it and assign more resources to it once it is understood that it's important to you. Don't have a Mission that can be separated into parts. It must be one concept. It must be one goal. There must be a single focus. Your life, in this case, will depend on it, so keep it simple if you want to have the best chance to survive.

Example: An infantry company has been assigned a hilltop to take possession of. There is in this a Mission, and there are missions. The missions, the sub-tasks, might be phrased this way: "1st Platoon will advance partway up the objective's north slope to fix the enemy's attention and distract them. 2nd Platoon will simultaneously maneuver to the right flank and, once the enemy has committed to dealing with 1st Platoon's advance, attack up the west side to the objective. 3rd Platoon will split heavy weapons section off to support 2nd Platoon, provide light fire support for 1st Platoon, and provide the reserve to exploit the breakthrough to the objective."

Those are missions, small 'm'. What's the Mission? TAKE THE HILL. Or even more simply put, WIN. Once the 'subconscious' of the company internalizes the Mission, the actual steps to achieving it are worked out based on knowledge and experience. The process of supporting and achieving the Mission becomes automatic, instinctive, and adaptable to circumstance once the Mission is properly internalized. It will work the same way with you. Determine your Mission and accept it. Your 'command staff', your subconscious and conscious mind, will take your knowledge and experience and adapt it to the demands of the encounter.

For best effect, I believe that the Mission should have a 'Why?' answer attached to it. There must be a reason why you want to accomplish your Mission. Captain Miller wanted to go home to his wife. Why? Because he loved her and wanted to see her again; because she needed his support and needed for him to come home. Private Ryan wanted to be a Good Man. Why? Because someone who had died to keep him alive had wished him to do so with his last words; because he wished to honor the sacrifice made for his sake.

SURVIVE, or WIN, are simple, easily understood Missions, but without a 'Why', I don't believe it's enough by itself to just have the Mission. I don't believe the subconscious, especially, will grasp the centrality and importance of the Mission unless a solid 'Why?' answer is attached to it. Because for most of us, simple existence is not enough. For most of us, simple victory is not enough. There has to be something 'to' existence or victory for most of us. That's what the 'Why' is. So increase your chances of winning by making sure you have one.

That's the basics of making and having a Mission as I see it. Closing this subject out, let me say one more thing: You may fail anyway. There are no guarantees. Understanding the need for the counter-attacking mindset, having a Mission, knowing Why, none of these things will guarantee your survival in the face of unexpected assault. It did not save Miller in the movie; it has not saved people in Reality; it may not save you.

Nonetheless, I very firmly believe that you are more likely to survive having these things than if you don't. I believe as firmly that to neglect these things is to increase the risk that you will not survive the fight. So I urge you to start now and get these things. Get them inside of you and make them part of you. Don't just decide that you will fight and win. DECIDE that you will FIGHT and WIN, and know WHY you're going to.

More than you may know beyond you depends on your doing that.

YES, YOU CAN BUY SKILL
You just can't do it the way you might think you can.

Comments about what I write about gunfighting and what I did as a gunfight instructor are almost always helpful. Even the negative or dismissive ones usually provide some useful information. One of the comments that followed an article titled "What They're Not Telling You About Point Shooting" (You can go to Part Two of the book now and read it if you like.) is an example of this. One comment that told me something was:

"Point shooting? Get a laser sight and not worry about where it's pointed."

What that comment told me was:

That some of you really think (consciously or not) that Gadgets = Skill.

THAT COULD BE A FATAL MISTAKE

There are "Gadgets" and there is "Equipment". A "Gadget" as I'll use the term here is anything a person gets with the idea, subconsciously or not, that it will give them a skill or capability they don't already have. That includes a gun, something you put on or in a gun, something you do to a gun, or something you get to use with the gun. It would be anything obtained under the delusion that just having that item will give you something, some kind of capability or competency, without much, if any, effort.

"Equipment" is anything you get that makes it easier to do something you already do or that adds to a capability you already have. The same item that is a Gadget in one shooter's hands is Equipment when used by another shooter.

A 2,000-dolllar custom-tuned handgun purchased by someone who had yet to take their first shooting class and furthermore was not going to take one is a Gadget. (You could say the same thing for any gun that someone bought with no intention of training or practicing with it.) For someone with good shooting skill and prior training the same gun is Equipment. Any rifle and scope combination I purchased with the expectation that I could take them out of the box, put them together, zero the scope, and then go home expecting there-ever-after to put hits on a torso-size target out to six hundred yards at will would be a Gadget for me. I don't yet have the training I need to go with it. For my friend who was a Marine rifle instructor or someone who has gone through instruction about long-range shooting, it is Equipment.

The difference between a Gadget and Equipment as I define it, then, is the person that's using it and their intentions and expectations about it.

Since they were specifically mentioned, take Lasers for example: Buy a laser, put it on the gun (or get one that already has a laser on it), maybe zero it, and rest easy. All you have to do is put the dot on the bad guy and pull the trigger after that…

…unless you're in bright light and can't see the dot…or it's foggy or smoky and the laser can't get through...or he's outside the laser's range...or you miss the switch...or it doesn't come on the one time you have to have it...or you haven't practiced sighting with the laser the right way and focus on finding the dot on the target instead of focusing on the target and letting the dot appear, which slows you down so much you never get the shot off because the bad guy kills you while you're still hunting for it...

(Yes, it can happen. Shooters new to lasers tend to treat the laser like a front sight, shifting focus from the target to the dot. They end up 'hunting' for it, which makes their first shot slower compared to the standard sights they are used to shooting with. Slower first shot makes for higher risk of injury or death. Proper training overcomes this.)

In other words, if you don't have the baseline skill to back the laser up with, it's a Gadget and you could be setting yourself up for trouble (Maybe with a capital 'T', maybe not, but still trouble just the same.).

Another example is the gun I'm wearing as I write this: A Glock 19 with a Trijicon RMR mounted on the slide. FAR superior to any non-military laser system I've ever seen or read about or heard of. It has extended my effective range, my practical accuracy, and reduced the time it takes to make a precision shot. It has done this for others as well. For me, and them, it's not a Gadget, it's Equipment.

But...it has not given me anything that I didn't have before I got it, and it hasn't given me anything that I couldn't get (in the way of base capability) without it. The RMR does not shoot the gun for me and does not guide the bullet. I still have to drive the gun level and under control to the target, I still have to have the proper grip, I still have to have eye-to-sight alignment, and I still have to work the trigger properly. I still, in other words, have to know how to correctly shoot the gun just like everybody else does. The RMR is Equipment for me because it enhances existing capability, not because it gives me something I don't have already.

TSD Combat Systems slide with Trijicon RMR mounted on a G19. (This particular variant is no longer produced.) Have you done what it takes to wring the full performance potential out of this kind of setup? Have you done what it takes to make this Equipment and not just another Gadget in your collection?

The laser doesn't come with skill included. The RMR doesn't come with skill included. The thousand-plus-dollar gun doesn't come with skill included.

No Gadget does.

That's the truth of it. Ignore that truth at peril of your life.

I said I'd tell you how you could buy skill. If the Gadget doesn't give you capability, how do you get it?

Simple: Don't buy the Gadget before you **buy training**.

I repeat: **You want skill? GET TRAINING FIRST.**

Training gets you skill that turns a Gadget into Equipment. Training gets you skill that stays with you whether you have that Equipment or not. Training gives you skill that you can use

Equipment to extend. Training gets you skill that doesn't go away if the Equipment breaks. **Training gets you Skill.**

THIS. This is how you buy skill. With money and time and effort on the line at a class with a good instructor. No gadget is going to give you what these men are getting out of their investment.

Gadgets don't.

A secondary benefit of taking training is that you will see and have a chance to work with various Gadgets and Equipment, and you can get the benefit of others' experience with them. Watching how various things perform and help their owners, or not, can help you greatly in your own decisions about what you should pick up and what you should not touch. It will help you decide down the road what Gadgets you should avoid, and what Equipment you should be looking to get.

The main thing, though, is the skill you get. Skill that doesn't need mounts, doesn't need batteries, doesn't have conditions or limits to its operation that you don't have already or place on it, and that will last as long as you do and as long as you do just a bit of maintenance work on them from time to time.

Skill you can buy.

That's the secret.

I'm not against add-ons, enhancements, or equipment, ladies and gentlemen. I have some and will be getting more. I recommend them to others on an ongoing basis (Prime example: I think everybody as they are able to should get an RMR mounted. Red dots are Game Changers, guys. *Game. Changers.*) Equipment is useful, Equipment will help you do things, and Equipment will help you do things easier. *But nothing will do anything that you can't already do or learn to do*, even if it is harder to do it without that thing. Nothing comes with skill in the box as a no-cost bonus.

Want to <u>do</u> better?

Want to BE better?

Get the training sooner, add Equipment—not Gadgets—later. Simple as that.

PATTERNING CHAOS
Learn the pattern, practice the pattern, integrate the pattern, become the pattern, discard the pattern.

The Fight.

Havoc. Confusion. Distraction. The Fog of your very own, intensely personal WAR. Solid waste impacting the forced-air distribution system. Pain and fear and anger. Adrenaline dumping to the bloodstream. Tunnel vision and auditory exclusion and tricks on your perception and thinking and memory. All of that and it feels like more.

Chaos, let's call it. Entropy focused in time and space, entropy squared where you're at and when you're there. The three laws of thermodynamics rolling into a point and hitting you square in the head and heart, driving into your world at a time and place of the bad guy's choosing and, as much as he can make it, under his control.

Your mission if that happens, whether you decide to accept it or not, is to manage that sudden Chaos enough to be the one that goes home when the fight is over and your life has returned to its normal and invisibly-entropic state. Your mission is to not just survive, but to regain and impose order through the Chaos, enough order so that the bad guy's plan suffers its own sudden and unexpected entropic onset and collapses on him.

Put more plainly, you want to <u>win</u> the fight you didn't know was coming and you want to <u>win it decisively</u>.

How do you do that? By planning and preparation and practice and training. Everybody knows that.

Everybody also knows that the fight is fluid, the fight is chaotic, and you can't predict when the fight will come or how the fight will develop and happen. You won't know where, you won't know when, you won't know who, you won't know how many, you won't know…

By definition, you can't <u>really</u> expect the unexpected. That's why it's called 'the unexpected' in the first place, right?

So how do you prepare for something you won't know about?

Here is a paradox of preparing for the fight: To be able to handle Chaos, you have to learn about Order. To deal with what is fluid, you must first build a foundation of and on that which is solid.

You have to learn the Patterns. You simply will not fight as well without them as you will if you have learned them well enough to discard them. And that is another paradox of the fight: To have the best chance of winning decisively, you must yourself fight without a pattern, and you can't do that without first learning what those patterns are.

If Combat Is Chaos, though, why do we have to learn Patterns? Why can't we learn a bunch of techniques (some of which are themselves Patterns, mind you) and then apply them 'on the fly' as needed?

Patterns teach us concepts and principles that stretch over, organize, and direct us and the techniques we learn. An example: Roger Phillips' 'Drawstroke Continuum' that he teaches in his shooting courses. The pattern we learn is the drawstroke to a range of places, planes, orientations, and directions. The concepts and principles we learn include such things as driving the gun to the target, extending the gun only as far as is safe (from a snatch attempt), and staying under the master eye or visual center throughout. Even learning a basic to-the-front X-count drawstroke, you learn those things sometimes without knowing you are learning those things. All I remember doing before my first with course Roger was a normal drawstroke, but once he had explained things and we started running, it became a serviceable multi-directional, multi-level, multi-range variable draw that accommodated itself to whatever direction we needed it to and that has continued to refine itself over time. I didn't learn a different drawstroke for each specific direction, I learned the Pattern well enough to get the Principles and Concepts integrated and then dropped it (keeping the Principles and Concepts) when it didn't go to exactly the direction and level I needed to go to. You can, and will, do the same if you will only apply yourself to that kind of focused training.

Patterns give us automatic responses that start us acting while we're still surprised. There is a saying about finding yourself in a survival situation that goes something like: "Do SOMETHING even if it's wrong!" The idea is to start yourself moving and acting in order to keep yourself from stopping either because you panic and freeze or because you over-think the situation and hesitate to do anything that's not near-perfect. The same principle can apply to the much smaller time-scales involved in a fight for life. Patterns integrated and made automatic can get us moving when the tendency might be to stop until our mind processes the input of the attack. The repetitive practice of the pattern gives our subconscious, the 'monkey brain' that takes over in those moments, a familiar thing. You know what to do without being conscious of it, and as you're getting caught up consciously, you're taking action, even if it's not perfect. That gives you a chance to get 'on course' while it throws off the attacker's planning about how things will go. You catch up, you get ahead, you win. Without learning the pattern, the risk is increased that you freeze while you're assessing things. You fall further behind and you lose. Better to have the 'automatic' built in somewhere.

The Patterns we learn are sometimes all we need to Win. There are many cases where just the first move, or the setup for the first move, whether that's drawing the weapon but not using it to the first automatic block/deflection/evasion and counterstrike, will change the attacker's mind about continuing. Starting the pattern you have learned and made automatic starts your mind and spirit on their way to 'fighting' mode as well. The physical reflects on the mental which alters the physical again, and on and on. By assuming the 'attitude' that a particular Pattern forces on you, you may tell the attacker that you're more of a risk than others and make them decide to break away. You go home unharmed. That's a Win.

Patterns are the basis of the improvisation that we need in the fight. There are a limited number of chords and notes in music, but look at the music that is generated from that. There are only three primary colors that, mixed together various ways, produce all the hues and tones we see and use. The human body only moves in certain ways over certain ranges, and the most efficient ways to move are limited, but that has not limited the sports and the martial arts that have been developed to use those movements over those ranges. The patterns we learn in the beginning are what we will use in the near-continuous adaptation to the specific threat and the specific fight we may or will face—and I can all but guarantee that we will have to adapt, to modify and add and subtract from and combine those basic patterns to meet the demands of the moment. Broad similarities? Surely so. But even fighting the same opponent in the same place, something is always different, something will always demand at least some variation and adaptation to the demands of the instant. If it happens in controlled environments—the ring, the Octagon, the dojo—how much more likely is it to happen in the parking lot at 8pm?

Patterns, then, are *important*, and not just something to grit your teeth and bear until the instructor gets to the really neat stuff. Because…and trust me on this one…you won't do the really neat stuff nearly as well unless you've given more than a cursory nod and some lip service to the fundamental concepts and principles that Patterns teach you. And unless you can do the fundamentals and the basics well and almost forgetfully when you're on the range shooting straight up and straight ahead, you risk not being able to do them in the drugstore parking lot at 8:30 in the evening when you're caught between two cars and the guy on your left with the big knife.

Musashi might have put it this way: Study the Way, make the Way part of you, become the Way, forget the Way and be what you really were in the beginning. I say it this way: Learn the Patterns, integrate the Patterns, make the Patterns natural, forget the Patterns, and so become more comfortable in Chaos. Either way you put it, if you do this—and it doesn't take as much effort and time as you may think to—you will still end up being able to defend yourself and destroy your enemies far better and more quickly than you could before.

And that's the bottom line to all of this, isn't it?

WHAT DO YOU KNOW?

Two people, both instructors with a lot of time on the books, once posted in the same thread on a gun forum and ended their posts with the same question:

"But what do I know?"

A day or two later, I find myself pondering this very thing, because it's a great question.

What DO you know?

And it leads to some very useful follow-ups:
Is what you know useful?

Is what you know <u>relevant</u>?

Is what you know <u>current</u>?

Does what you know actually help you or someone else?

I work in the Information Technology field. I'm used to asking those questions to myself on an almost daily basis. And I'm used to the answers sometimes being, in order: Not Enough, Not So Far, Not To This Situation, Not At This Time. When I get those answers, I'm used to working on getting the knowledge I need to change the answers so that I can solve the problems.

As a student of the fight, I need to be asking the same questions to myself periodically. If I can't answer the questions any better than I do sometimes in my IT work, I need to start working on changing the answers as quickly as possible.

You need to be doing the same thing. If you're a student of the fight (and if you're reading this I assume that you are), you need to ask the same questions and look for the right answers to them. To not ask and answer these questions for yourself is to risk not knowing what you need to know at the time and place you need to know it. To not ask and answer these questions for yourself is to risk your safety and the safety of others. Life might depend on having the right answers to these questions.

As an instructor, I think I have not just a personal need, but an <u>obligation</u> to ask myself these questions periodically. I believe that <u>every</u> instructor should feel the same obligation, because we ask these questions not just for ourselves, but for our students. And not having the very best answers we can have to these questions is a potential risk to the safety of everyone we teach. It is <u>imperative</u> that we not only stay current on the threats students face—<u>today</u>—and the most effective tactics and techniques, but that we also examine what we know already to make sure that the knowledge and experience we have is still relevant and useful to everyone we pass it on to in our classes.

"Sometimes a teacher, always a student."

It's not just a nice quote or catch-phrase, even if you're not an instructor. Every gun-bearer that I know of has other people that know they carry, and most if not all of them have had people ask for help and advice about guns and shooting and self-defense. It may not be phrased as "What do you know?", but by word or observation, every one of us answers that question for someone else.

It's not just the teachers who teach, and it's not just the students who learn.

Roger Phillips, founder of Fight Focused Concepts, for example: The man knows point shooting. Lots of people know that. What some people don't know is that the man also knows what is often called the Modern Technique of the Pistol, or MT, the system of fighting with a handgun developed by Jeff Cooper. He has a LOT of learning and practice time on the clock in MT.

So why isn't he teaching MT?

One weekend, Roger and a bunch of other high-level MT practitioners were asked, *"What do you know?"* by a series of Force-on-Force scenarios. The answer was, *"Not enough."* Everybody had problems solving the problems presented in the scenarios. Everybody started doing things to solve the problems that weren't part of the MT knowledge base that they knew so much of.

Roger saw that and experienced that and afterwards asked himself questions like: "What that I know already was useful? What was not? What do I need to know about the fight that MT didn't teach me?"

Roger became a student again. He studied point shooting in all its aspects, he studied movement, he took instruction, he worked with others, and he practiced himself. He answered the questions that were asked that weekend and that he asked himself afterwards. He did not totally discard MT, but by asking the follow-up questions he was able to keep what was relevant and current out of MT and merge it with what he was learning about point shooting.

So he answered those questions and then the student became a teacher.

But—*and this is Important*—he did not stop asking those questions to himself. And so, the teacher is still as student—one who learns from students who don't know they are teaching him.

Cut to Advanced Point Shooting Progressions, a class Roger designed and was teaching when he was a Specialist Instructor at Suarez International. After taking the Point Shooting Progressions course that he also taught at the time, students were asking a variation of the basic question—"What <u>else</u> do you know?"—and Roger answered it with this course.

I took either the second or third one he taught after he had developed the course. Course description said, "Bring a back-up gun. You will work with that during the course." (I don't call it a back-up any more. Now I just call it a second gun.)

Now I had to answer a question. What do I know about second guns? I looked at what I knew and what I could learn before the course, I did some thinking and experimentation and qualification, and I came up with this answer you see in the photo here.

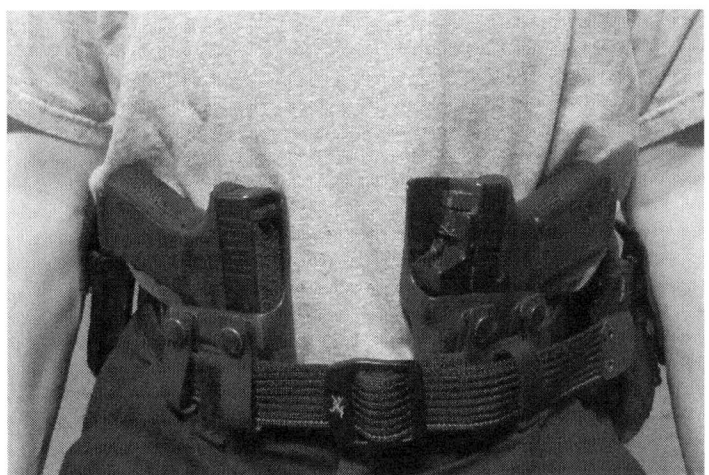

It's an old idea that has been done since, probably, handguns got small enough to stick in a belt or sash. (It doesn't have to be new to be current or relevant or useful. It's a mistake to think that way.) Roger used mirror-image guns and rigs in training when he was a Modern Technique practitioner. He recalled this as he observed me running the course (I was the first one to use this setup in APSP.) He observed me answering the second-gun question this way, and other students answering the second-gun question the way they did. He decided that I had a good answer (Sometimes there will be only one best answer and sometimes there will be many answers, all of which are good.) and he worked on the concept himself, and then the man who was a student who became a teacher who is still a student went back to being a teacher again. He talked to others about the concept and he wrote about it on the Warrior Talk forum. Others picked up the idea and looked to see if it answered their own questions about carrying and accessing a second gun.

The next time Roger did his APSP course, half the class was carrying in what is now called a dual-appendix setup. Some people now carry this way regularly while others use this setup whenever they put on a second gun, but not all the time. This setup answers questions for them like it did for the first man that ever stuck a second pistol in his belt. For others, the answer is a different setup, but the questions remain the same.

Questions that generate answers that generate questions that generate answers that generate…

Students being teachers being students being…

If you're a student, I think it very important that you start and continue this kind of query-response cycle.

If you're an instructor, I believe that it is all but imperative that you do.

So:

WHAT DO YOU KNOW?

Answer the question.

LABELS
Sheepdog? Wolf? Wolfhound? None of the above? Does it matter? <u>Should</u> it matter? Maybe. Sometimes. Here's why.

Who's behind you?

That question was actually the original title I had for this part. I ask it because for most of us, even if we are alone and isolated when an attack starts, there is someone, somewhere, who is depending on us to stay up and stay alive and to go home to them. Sometimes, I think, some of us have different attitudes about what we'll do and how we'll do it if the fight comes to us when we're with those we care about, as opposed to what we'll do and how we'll do it if we're alone at the time. I don't believe you should forget that you're learning to fight, preparing for the fight, and training to fight to protect someone else besides yourself, whether they're three feet or three thousand miles behind you at the time.

That concept fits the idea that is labeled as 'Sheepdog'. Some use that term, as described in the section 'On Sheep, Wolves, and Sheepdogs' in the book *On Combat* by Lt. Col Dave Grossman, to describe those who chose to go about armed and ready to resist those who would bring evil to those who are good. You, the sheepdog, have a group…a 'flock'…and you are on guard for them. Whether they are there, close to you, to guard is irrelevant to the fact that you are on guard for them. You protect yourself when you're alone because protecting yourself protects them too.

Some people in the self-defense world scoff at the use of the term 'Sheepdog' to denote a defender of any kind, or of the use of any label to denote a role such as the one we adopt in defense of ourselves and others. I think they may be mistaken about doing this. I think labels can be useful and may be (sometimes) necessary. Labels are word-symbols and mental keys to imagery and emotion and lists of attributes that we tie, positively or negatively, to the label. Labels represent the list of attributes that we want to adopt and maintain and strengthen. We remember the label easier than we can remember the list of attributes that it represents, and if we 'tie in' to the label mentally and emotionally, we can use the label to bring up the attributes and capabilities we need when we need them. The label, in some cases, becomes the foundation, the rock that we stand on and drive off of as we go to meet the challenge we are facing, or the wall at our back that stiffens us against that which cannot be allowed to pass. But understand it's not the label itself that does that. We have to develop the attributes and talents and capability that the label represents to us, or else the label is a lie. But in the times when we are threatened with our own doubts and forget our own capability to deal with the challenge, the label can be the key to remembering what we really are and what we have worked to become and what we can do to meet that challenge.

The words, "I AM (INSERT LABEL HERE)" can have power beyond imagination or comprehension by those who have not actually seen their effect.

BUT: As labels are positive things, they can also be negative things. Some ways a label can hurt and not help you would be: If you take the wrong label for yourself (I'm not a Sheepdog for example. It would limit me to try to be just that.); if you make the mistake of thinking that taking the label gives you the attributes it represents. (Like some who think that a piece of equipment is a substitute for skill, some think that a label, either one they pick up or one given to them, awards them the attributes and skill without them having to work for it. The realization of the mistake where we live in the self-defense/fight-for-life world is often painful and sometimes fatal); or when we hang on to a label for too long.

The last point merits a separate paragraph. Not everybody needs a label, and not everybody needs to hold on to a label forever. I dare to say that no one should seek to remain within the boundaries prescribed by some labels and that everyone should strive to move beyond any label they take on or are given with the goal of becoming simply everything they are again. Miyamoto Musashi, he who is called sometimes the Sword-Saint of Japan, spoke first of elemental labels—Ground, Water, Fire, Wind—and then of the Void, which both encompasses the others and at the same time is none of them. Masaaki Hatsumi, in his earlier writing and teaching about what is now called Bujinkan Budo Taijutsu, spoke of those same elements, each one encompassing certain characteristic of attitude as well as technique, and then of Void, where all was encompassed and all was discarded at the same time. What these two masters of their respective disciplines spoke of, we should be striving to become…both with, and without, defining labels.

In the same way we initially learn patterns to learn concepts and then (hopefully) grow to the point where we discard the patterns and are able to adapt the concepts to whatever the fight brings to us, so also we may initially adopt or accept labels in order to help us adopt and maintain helpful and necessary characteristics and attributes. The danger is that we become too comfortable inside of that label and never expand beyond the definitions it imposes. Then, when something demands something else, some other attribute or characteristic of us, we are faced with defeat, with failure, and perhaps even with death.

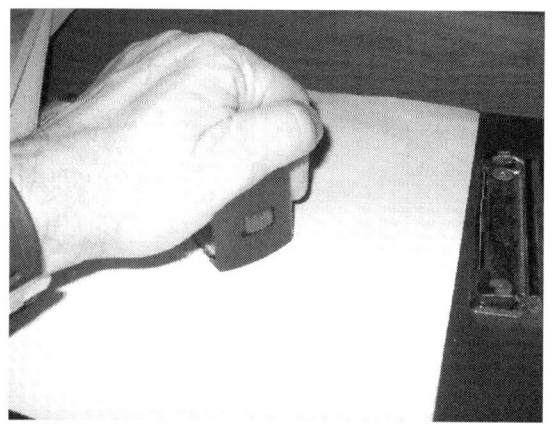

If the sheet of paper were <u>you</u>, what would it be stamped on it? What label would it leave as representative of what you are and what you do now? Or would it leave anything at all?

"DAMMIT, JIM, I'M A DOCTOR, NOT A...!!!!"

But if McCoy had *really* been *exactly* what his label said he was and nothing else, there are times when Captain and crew would not have survived to go on to the next episode, would they?

As the fictional Dr. McCoy had his labels but didn't allow them to limit him, neither should you. As he took the label and used it when it was to his advantage, so should you. And as he discarded that label when he needed to and when it was best to do so, so should you.

Labels, like guns and knives, are tools. Pick them up when they're best for the job. Put them down when you're finished with them. Know when you have the right one for what you need to do, and when you don't. And work to be able to use any of them by not needing any of them to be what you are.

The people behind you are counting on you to do that.

BEING LIKE JOHN WAYNE CAN'T BE ALL BAD

You sometimes hear or read someone being cautioned about having or adopting a "John Wayne attitude", or someone else will say that they're not "some kind of Rambo" as if they know of someone who is or thinks they are.

Let's look at that for a moment. What does it mean to <u>have</u> a "John Wayne attitude" or to <u>be</u> "some kind of Rambo"? Looking at the movie-actions of those various characters, this is what I see:

They prepared by prior training and/or were prepared by previous experience to do what they did. The preparation is either implied or stated at some point in each character's storyline. Prior preparation or experience was present and sufficient for what they needed or wanted to do.

They had reasons for resorting to violence. Whether those reasons were good or appropriate in our judgment is open to question, but unless I missed something somewhere, the fact that they had a reason for resorting to violence is not. I don't recall any instances of the characters as portrayed just 'going off'. It may have been the fulfillment of a mission (personal or official or both), it may have been a response to some provocation, but there was nonetheless a reason in each case.

They did not always kill even when they resorted to violence. Their standards for whether they killed or not may have been imposed from outside or composed from inside, but they did have standards for what they did, and how much they did, to any target of their violence. Even when they did kill, they didn't always kill everybody 'in the room' so to speak. Their violence, lethal or non-lethal, was (relatively) controlled and directed.

Nonetheless:

They accepted the fact that somebody at some point was going to (or was likely to) die because of what they did.

(Pay attention to this one, because this is what I think makes other people so inclined to make this a caution or an insult.)

Whether these characters set out to kill somebody (or – bodies) from the get-go or whether it happened in the course of their doing something else, they understood and accepted that somebody was at least very likely if not certain to die by their hands. They may not have anticipated a death in the course of their task or mission, but they did appear to have an accommodation of some sort with the idea of being the cause of another's death.

In this last point especially, these fictional characters were ahead of some, perhaps many, of the non-LE/non-military gun-carrying population of the United States, and maybe even of a goodly number of the professional gun-carriers that are employed in and by this country. I wonder if that mental preparation by some doesn't make those that haven't thought about it nervous or even a little scared.

It's not conscious, most of the time, but it can be close enough to the surface that if someone does talk about dealing with death personally dealt, some will feel guilty because they haven't done it and/or nervous, maybe even afraid, of those who have, and then somebody gets a warning about having a 'John Wayne attitude' or 'going all Rambo'.

It is also something that I believe should be dealt with, if you haven't already, or else it may get you killed.

If you're reluctant, even subconsciously, to deal with a death at your hands, you may hesitate. You may not even realize you've slowed the draw or the shot or something else down because of that reluctance-driven hesitation. You won't consciously <u>want</u> to slow down, you won't <u>intend</u> to slow down, but you <u>will</u>. And then it will be too late, and you will die.

Now, you do read about people who shoot, and sometimes kill, attackers that I bet never considered the idea that they would ever be the cause of death of anybody. So, yes, you can say that it's not absolutely necessary and you would be correct in saying that.

But consider this: How many good people are dead now because they hesitated to maybe kill someone? And how many good people are at least greatly disturbed, if not completely devastated, because they did not prepare ahead of time for the possibility that they might end up killing someone?

Yes, the odds of actual death by gunshot nearly anywhere in the US is less than fifty percent--I believe the actual average is about forty. So about sixty percent or more of those shot live through the shooting. Your chances here are better than average that your shot won't kill the attacker.

It's not zero, though. It's nowhere close enough to be zero to be confident about it. So we're back to being like so many of John Wayne's characters and starting to deal with the idea of being responsible for a justifiable homicide. I'm not asking you to be eager to kill. I'm not asking you to look forward to shooting someone to death. I'm not sure if a population of gun-bearers all excited about maybe getting a chance to drill somebody through the heart and head would work very well. It's not really why we carry, either. Is it?

But I don't want any of you reading this to hesitate at the moment when you need to shoot, and I don't want you to dissolve into uselessness to yourself or your family if you do have to shoot someone and find out you shot them dead. There are trainers and experts in various fields that will tell you that it's inevitable that you do, that taking the life of an attacker will at least hurt you a lot and may destroy you. *That is <u>not</u> necessarily the case. It <u>doesn't</u> happen every time to everyone and <u>it doesn't have to happen to you</u>.*

To be sure of making the experts wrong, though, you need to prepare for the mental encounter like you prepare for the physical encounter. You need to set yourself mentally and emotionally like you do physically. Like physical preparation, it doesn't guarantee you come out whole and unharmed. As you could still die in the fight, you could still suffer in the realization of having killed. I strongly believe, though, that mental preparation will raise the odds the way physical preparation does, and that considering this aspect of the fight will help you go home after the fight <u>completely</u> whole, in body, in heart, and in mind.

I'm all for adopting a John Wayne attitude or even being a little like Rambo, if it will help you do that.

GETTING TO GRIPS WITH A DIFFERENT HAMMER
Prepare to be able to use the tools you have, not the ones you prefer.

These two things are related:

What I call the 'hammer and nail syndrome'.

The fact that I only did half the workout that I had planned to do today.

Here's why:

The 'hammer and nail syndrome' used to be very prevalent in the population of those who regularly carry handguns for self-defense. It is still quite common to find it in the general population, especially in those who have not received some kind of inoculation against it, whether that be through direct experience, attention to the lessons taught by others' experiences, or through training by some, though not all, instructors and schools. The syndrome takes its name from the adage, "If all you have is a hammer, every problem starts to look like a nail."

Thus, if all you have is a gun, the syndrome turns everything, every serious attack at the least, into a 'gun problem' requiring a gun to solve it.

Somehow.

Easy to see how the mix-up occurs. If you're facing someone with a knife or a club or a rock in his hand, you're facing a lethal-force threat. That allows for, if not requires, a lethal-force response.

What it doesn't allow for, under certain conditions, is a lethal-force response using a firearm.

It's a simple enough idea to try out. Get a 'blue gun', an Airsoft gun or toy gun, or disable your firearm (several ways to do that). Give someone a training knife or soft club and have them attack you from three feet away....

"Hey! I'm in Condition Yellow at all times! They wouldn't get that close to me!"

Lie to me if you want to, but don't lie to yourself. Nobody is 'on' all the time. Nobody. Not you, not me, not the highest-speed-lowest-drag operator in the known universe. No-bah-dee. Okay?

If you insist on continuing the self-deception, though, then understand that there are situations, circumstances, and environments that could put you into close proximity with someone who makes you nervous without allowing you distance or avoidance. If they then attack suddenly, you're back to the close-in square-one situation I'm talking about right now.

Tell you what, though—you can run this test two ways if it will make you feel better. No, make that three ways:

Gun in hand and pointed at the attacker who is two or three

feet, arms-reach, away. Attacker will initiate.

Gun in holster with your hand on it, cover cleared. Attacker will initiate. Variation: Gun in hand in covert ready position out of sight of attacker.

Gun under cover as normal, your hands up between you and attacker. Attacker will initiate.

Variation to last two runs: Attacker keeps weapon hidden and engages you in conversation before initiating a draw and attack.

Obviously, two of these runs will not replicate the fact that, in reality, the attacker would normally not know you had a weapon. Your test attacker can act like it enough to give you some results to consider, though. Speaking of results, let me predict the most likely findings:

In the majority of the runs, the best you'll get is a tie. (And if you're okay with a tie, let me suggest two things: Make very sure you have a lot of insurance to support your family, and consider the epitaph, *"Yeah, but he's dead too!"* for your grave marker.) With the weapon in hand and pointed, you may get lucky and get a clear win every so often. Put them all together though, and look at them with brutal honesty, and you'll see that even having the gun out does not guarantee a win.

And <u>not</u> having the gun out—<u>unless you have additional tools to 'fix' the situation with</u>—means that you're really in trouble.

To keep you from getting too warm and fuzzy by thinking that all you have to do is maintain distance (in case you missed my earlier commentary about your self-deception habits), run those tests again, backing the attacker up two or three feet at a time. This is also a good way to determine your limits of action and reaction and the limits you should place on suspicious people and their behavior before you take some kind of action, violent or not, to remove yourself or resolve the situation.

And if you <u>can't</u> enforce those limits, and they <u>do</u> get in close and launch an attack, you need to be able to fight <u>without</u> the gun until you get to a position where you can get the gun to fight with.

Combatives. MMA. Martial Arts. Self-Defense techniques. Call it whatever you want, you need to have it available. It doesn't have to be fancy, it doesn't have to be complicated, and it doesn't have to get you through a three-round match in the Octagon. It just has to give you enough time to work to an escape or an access to a better weapon.

It just has to keep you alive, in other words.

Because even 'gun problems' are not always gun problems in the beginning. Sometimes they're 'got nothing but my hands and my skills' problems that you have to convert to gun problems the hard and fast way.

And to have the best chance of succeeding with whatever you know, you need a base of strength and speed and flexibility and stamina. You need to be able to generate power for as long as you need it and have enough energy to run away with after you're loose (if you can and if that is the best answer).

You need to be in good condition, in other words.

(Some of you were wondering when I was going to bring the workout into this. Now you know.)

You need to be in as good a condition as you can be, practically speaking, that is. We have lives, we have families, we have things we have to do. So we need to be practical about time and space and expense, yes…but we need to be in good condition regardless, to the best of our abilities.

And yes, I know—some of us are old, some of us are hurt, some of us are worn, some of us are tired, some of us are sick, some of us are more than one of these things.

Some of us, in other words, are what the predators of the human world are looking for. Conditioning will help to change what they see. Even if it doesn't, conditioning will help us avoid the fate of other prey.

Would you rather eat, or be eaten? Would you rather make the meal, or be the meal? Prey, or predator? Victim, or victor? (Survival is a win; escape is a win; going home is a win, whether the bad guy does or not.)

It doesn't have to be hard or complex. Like non-gun defense, conditioning can be simple and easy in planning if not in effort. Not a lot of gear needed, either; you may be surprised at what you can do with just your bodyweight. Start simple and slow, learn to gauge how your body is responding (it takes time, but it's important in the advanced stages to be able to do that), plan the in-betweens and the nutritional support (sounds better than diet, doesn't it?) like you plan the workouts. No need to spend hours on it and no need to try and change everything at once. A step at a time, a change at a time, and one day you realize you've gone a thousand miles.

To be the best defender you can be, you need to be considering the best way to us all of these tools.

A couple of things, though. You have to decide to do this. Repeatedly. Even when you don't feel like it (when you're physically able to do it; training when you're really sick or hurt isn't going to help you). Repeatedly. You have to commit to it. Repeatedly.

Because as long as you want to not be the meal, you'll need to keep working at it.

So: Where do you want to be on the food chain?

Answer while you can, before someone else gives you an answer you don't want to hear.

IN CONSIDERATION OF THE ACTIVE SHOOTER*

There have been active-shooter incidents. There will be more. Some of you are pretty sure of what you'll do if evil ever comes to visit like that. Some of you are worried and wondering what you're supposed to do against that.

So let's consider some concepts.

For one thing, *much of what you already know can be applied* against an Active Shooter just as well as it can be applied against an armed robber. The same tactics, the same techniques, the same tools, the same decisions, the same will to win, the same training you would use against Joe Thug and Jane Thugget are applicable here as well.

Don't be fooled and don't fool yourself into thinking that this is some kind of unusual situation where little if anything that you already have applies. It is not.

That said, more training will help. Most of us don't have enough. And by training, I mean fight training, as opposed to shooting training. Yes, you need to learn how to shoot the gun. That's fundamental, and that's important. But you need to move quickly to learn how to fight with the gun. Start choosing your training opportunities accordingly.

Visualization it. Visualization is your friend. I don't mean idle day-dreaming or casual 'what-ifs' in your head. I mean the mental equivalent of the Star Trek Next Generation Holodeck. Set up the image, establish the players, start the production...you are the director and actor.

Look at the set-up, the movement, the angles, the actions, the reactions. See yourself acting correctly, hitting solidly, fighting, winning. If you're not feeling some emotional reaction and maybe a slight increase in pulse rate, think harder. Visualization is a proven tool to improvement, to competence, to survival. Properly done visualization that supplements real fight training will take you an exceedingly long way toward both competency and competence in the face of unexpected evil.

Finally, *understand the stakes*. This is not a normal crime. There is little if any chance that you can stop them with a warning or the simple display of a weapon. So far, most Active Shooters have not survived their assaults, whether it was because they killed themselves or were killed by others. You have to go with the historical evidence, and the historical evidence indicates that the Active Shooter does not intend to survive their attack.

They have walked in to that place with the idea that they are going to choose the time and place of their death, and of yours. Don't let them have that choice. Don't let them choose for you. Don't let them decide.

Be clear about this: The choice they offer will not be whether or not anyone lives or dies. The choice will be <u>who</u> dies, <u>where</u> they die, <u>when</u> they die. <u>You will have the opportunity and the chance to take that choice away from them</u>. You can deny them the last bit of absolute power they try to take before they die. The opportunity will be yours.

TAKE IT.

*For a further examination of the Active Shooter problem and response, consider my booklet "Facing The Active Shooter" available at Amazon.com.

PELVIC SHOTS AND BEING 'BATMAN WITH A GUN'

I've had reasons in the last few weeks to ponder the concept of the pelvic shot.

The pelvic shot as first resort re-surfaces every so often in gun-world conversation. It's not an outright bad idea--targeting the line roughly hip-to-hip to break the pelvic structure and make the attacker unable to walk or run. If it works, you get what the military calls a 'mobility kill'. The bad guy falls down and can't run you down or chase you if you run away. It's useful if the attacker is wearing body armor, going to the head or neck is contra-indicated for some reason, in clinch-range to avoid hitting your own striking/blocking/holding arm and hand, or when there is no better target to start with. It also could be fatal anyway, regardless of your intentions.

Good reasons to choose a pelvic (or other non-Center-Of-Mass) shot. Top: If that was good cover and they were stupid enough to give you the leg and hip like that, you would be wise to take that shot and not wait for COM to show itself. Bottom: Going low to avoid your own blocking or striking arm is not a bad idea, either.

(Note: I would not necessarily go for the strike against a gun coming out; I would be more likely to jam the gun against his body and move my pistol over that hand and shoot him in the chest or head. This is an illustration of a concept, not a recommendation of a specific tactic.)

We're back to my suspicion that far too few people who carry guns have faced the hard fact that they are carrying lethal-force weapons and that they will be employing lethal force in the eyes of the legal system whether they deliberately shoot to wound from the get-go or not. I've had reason, in the last few weeks, to wonder how many have really come to terms with that, at least enough not to hesitate if they have to shoot or go to pieces if the odds break against them and the attacker dies from their return fire.

The reason you do not want to train yourself to automatically default to a pelvic shot as a first resort. By the time you realize the error and over-ride your trained initial reaction, it would probably be too late.

I think this may be why the pelvic shot is attractive to some gun-carriers. It can offer the illusion that you can stop the attack and the attacker without it being as likely as a center-mass-shot of killing them in the process. (Never mind the profusion of blood vessels, the proximity of the lower part of the spinal cord, the nerve endings in the groin region that make it a lethal-force target whether you mean it to be or not.) It's the same kind of avoid-the-uncomfortable thinking, conscious and not, that loads a home-defense shotgun with rubber bullets or birdshot instead of buckshot, or the first round of a defensive handgun with snake shot.

I'll warn them. They'll see the gun. They'll hear it when I rack the twelve-gauge. I'll hurt them, make them stop. I'll stop them without killing them. They won't die, I won't have killed them. I won't have to think about killing them.

So you'll try that wounding shot. You'll go for the leg or pelvis and you'll make a good shot that stops them, but not from killing you.

Or you'll rack the shotgun from the end of the hall and they'll keep coming. You'll shoot, but the rubber pellets won't hurt enough or the birdshot won't penetrate enough, and they will keep coming. And you'll be dead and your family will be left with your murderer(s).

You can't be Batman with a gun. Simple as that.

Why bring up Batman? One, because Batman comes up nearly as much as Rambo and John Wayne in cautions and denials. Two, because like some people who carry guns in the Western world in general and the US specifically, Batman does his dead level best not to kill anybody even if they should be killed. (With one exception: My favorite Batman, the one in the series The Dark Knight Rises printed a number of years ago. In his mid-fifties and a bit crazy, that one was. Batmobile was built and armed like a World War One tank, the Batcopter was a Hind, and in one scene he did put a hostage-taker down permanently...with an M60...firing it one-handed...holding it like you hold a pistol at arm's length. But I digress...)

Now, I do wonder how many lawyers Batman kept employed to handle however many bad guys died accidentally from him beating on them. (You have to know, as hard as he treated them, that every single one of them did not go to jail with mild headaches and a few bruises here and there. Even comic book realities only allow for so much suspension of disbelief. On the other hand, you do have all those guys that can fly and whatnot...)

Now <u>unlike</u> Batman, we don't go hunting for bad guys to take down unless we're in one of the jobs that requires it. Most of us will be trying to avoid trouble, not look for it. And most of us won't, if we order our lives correctly, be found by it.

You get the point, though. Pelvic shots first up, rat shot first round, rubber bullets or birdshot, show them the gun and they'll fold, rack the shotgun and they'll wilt...deep, deep down, there it is, that idea that they won't have to die and if they do, you won't be the one that has to kill them.

And except that this is reality and not a comic-book environment crafted to allow for even bad guys to come out alive, maybe you won't. But, it being reality, maybe you will.

GET USED TO IT. Do what you have to do to get past the hesitation, to bring the subconscious wishes into the open and expose them for what they are, to avoid possible death at the hands of someone who will NOT hesitate and HAS come to terms with the killing of humans, to reduce if not eliminate the suffering and confusion that would otherwise be faced, not just by you alone, if you ever have to be the one that survives by making sure the other guy does not.

If you're going to carry a gun or have it close to hand at all, it is a very important consideration.

So start working on it, all of it, now. Don't expect it to come on its own like some do, don't put it off like some do. Make it part of your development and training just like you do your physical fight skills and cultivate it the way you do awareness of your surroundings. To be able to live through it--not just survive it, but live through it and after it--you need the total package.

Your life, not just your physical life but your whole life and the whole lives of others, could depend on it.

CAN YOU SHOOT SOMEBODY YOU _KNOW_?

There was once a thread on the Warrior Talk Internet forum (faded into history now, as all threads usually do) that was titled: "Can You Shoot The Cheerleader?" What the poster of the original article is doing is getting you to think about how an attacker is <u>not</u> always going to fit your idea of what an attacker looks like. There are ten-year-olds who have murdered and robbed, there are blonde-haired high-school-age girls that have robbed banks, there are older and younger men and women who have committed the full range of felony crimes. It is not just the eighteen-to-twenty-five males from the bad part of town that do these things, and to think only of them and to key only on them as you go about your preparation for counter-offensive action is a possibly fatal mistake.

So, I think, is not considering the idea that you might one day have to fire on a family member, a close friend or someone in a close friend's family, or someone else in the circle of people that you consider 'safe' and 'trusted', consciously or not.

You don't have to dwell on it for very long, but a little time spent answering this question might be a good idea:

Are you prepared to shoot and possibly kill an acquaintance, a co-worker of long-time association, a friend or member of a friend's family, or one of your own family members if it's necessary to save your own or another's life?

Let's be honest with ourselves: Most of our thinking, most of our training, is oriented toward defense from strangers or people little-known to us. We set ourselves on the assumption that our first true 'sight' of the attacker we'll shoot will be when they come at us or just before. We don't expect the sight picture to be framed around the face of someone we've worked with for years, someone we go to church with, someone we live with, the wife or husband or son or daughter of the neighbor(s) we had over for barbecue two weeks ago.

For the second time in my life, I have had to contemplate the possibility (not probability; different concepts there) that I might need to shoot someone that I am more than peripherally aware of. The most recent case is different from the first case, which is still in effect and which involves and even closer relationship. The central point is that in both cases, if it becomes necessary, I won't be pulling the gun and the trigger on a stranger.

This can present difficulties if you haven't thought it through ahead of time.

I believe I have the parameters set and will do what's necessary in both cases if it ever comes to that need for decision. I may turn out be wrong about that if the need actually comes upon me, but I've at least tried to get ready for the possibility.

Have you?

YOU <u>WILL</u> HAVE BAD DAYS AT THE RANGE

I went to the range very early (not long after sunrise, in fact) a while back with a mind to run some live fire drills to determine if the non-shooting practice at home was 'taking'. I have been very pleased in the last couple of range visits to find that an adjustment to the drawstroke had significantly reduced my not-moving time to first shot from under closed-front cover. I had been working a couple of things that I identified as issues with that and wanted to see if I had resolved them.

The first few simple dynamic drills, movement and draw to a single shot, did not go well. It's getting cold, I kept the coat on over the shirt, and had problems with clearance. That was fairly quickly resolved, however, and the next few minutes of move (not too hard or fast, focusing on the first step)/draw/shoot one-or-three drills went much better. No quarter-sized groups like I see other people do at Roger Phillips' point-shooting classes, but actually some better than I had seen previously.

Thus encouraged, I picked up the shot-timer to see what kind of progress I had made in the last few weeks. The answer: Not any. I was, in fact often .05 to .1 slower than my average of weeks past before I made the adjustment. Also, I was sometimes completely off the IDPA target from where I was...somewhere between five and seven yards, I didn't measure it.

You can get frustrated and discouraged and tell yourself how bad you're doing and how hopeless you are, or you can focus and direct that time and energy into determining what is wrong and correcting the problem. What are you going to do? DECIDE.

Not so encouraging, I say to myself.

Now, some people will tell you that you'll have these periods and you should just slow down and refocus and blow them off and don't let it get to you. Some people are able to do that. I'm not convinced that a lot of us can, though. I know it is more difficult for me to just ignore a sudden downturn. Ever said something like, "Come ON, man!" in that frustrated tone of voice to yourself? You know the voice I'm talking about. I caught myself doing that a few times this morning.

But you can't allow yourself to <u>keep</u> the discouragement either. And it can be detrimental, perhaps even dangerous in some senses, to just tell yourself you're having a bad day and ignore the mistakes and misses and think that you'll be okay and back up to speed next time. You at least want to ask yourself a few questions and check some things before you decide it's just an off day.

Pertinent questions include:

Do you notice something happening in more than one drill or variation of something you're practicing? When I started timing the drawstroke, I was having clearance problems like I was at the beginning of the movement drills I ran first thing. I wasn't clearing enough from the gun and clothing was snagging and dragging on the other things I keep on my belt. A longer shirt-tail wasn't helping much, either.

Is the error you're making consistent and repeatable? On the first shot with the right hand, I was consistently putting the shot left. One reason was bad placement of the finger on the trigger. Another reason I was able to identify was that I was not triggering the shot at the right point of extension. I was actually firing after the arm was fully extended. At speed, that means the hand is 'whipping' some from the sudden stop at extension. I was not driving the gun under control and breaking the shot just as or the instant before full extension.

If you slow down/focus on/smooth out the movement or technique, does it get better for you? When I ignored the focus on the target point and paid attention to breaking the shot at the right place (I started by simply pulling back to #2 or #3 position, then extending and breaking the shot a few times), I not only got a better feeling about the extension and the shot, I hit the right area on the target. When I slowed down and focused on clearing the shirt, I could see that I was not making proper contact and not pulling/ripping in the right directions. I could also see exactly where the other stuff on the belt was getting in the way like it had not been doing at home.

Has something changed in look or feel from the last time you were doing this movement/technique? This is a standard question we ask in the IT-support industry when troubleshooting a computer or network problem: What has changed? It may take someone else looking at you to tell, or you may can feel the change or see the results yourself like I did. When the difference is detected, the next step is to look for what exactly has changed. It's not enough to know that something is different. The beginning of a solution comes from knowing as surely as you can <u>what</u> is different from last time.

Now that you have some answers, you can work out some solutions. One thing to keep firmly in mind when you start adjusting things is: *If possible, change only one thing, preferably something small, at a time.* Make one change, test, evaluate; accept or discard the change; make another change, test, evaluate; repeat until the issue is resolved and improvement is seen.

That's what I did early today, and that's what I will continue to do at home. I could have come out of the range session this morning discouraged still and wondering if I had the right idea about this. What I did was recognize the discouragement setting in and channel it into help with the problem-solving. My way of beating the downer experience was to tell myself, "I'll not let you get me down--I'll show you! I'll find out what's wrong and I'll fix it!" And most of the emotion--not all, but most--became energy used to focus on what was going on and make notes about what had to be done.

Will it work to do that? I happen to believe it will. I intend to prove it next time I go out to shoot. And I believe the same process will work for you too.

EVERYBODY has bad days, guys. EVERYBODY. The difference is what some people do with them. Decide that you're going to be the one that makes the bad days good. Learn not just from the obvious mistakes, *learn from everything*, including an extended period of lower-than-average performance. Work the questions, work the answers, work the solutions, find the fix. I know you can do it because I've done it. If I can do it, any of you can do it too.

Right?

Good. Now get to work.

PART TWO: ART, SCIENCE, METHOD

WE USUALLY DO THIS BACKWARDS, DON'T WE?

We get the guns and we take the classes, we watch the videos and read the books, we learn the techniques and we practice the methods all before we begin to think about what we need to be thinking about. When it's covered in classes it's usually a short, small module compared to the rest of the curriculum. Mindset is first in importance, but second in actual consideration and/or acquisition for most of us because it's easier to start on the physical things and because the physical things are easier to see and to reach (in a way) and to teach (definitely).

Hopefully, the fact that you're at this point in the book means that you're considering or re-considering the most important part, even if you don't agree with my approach to it and even if you're not fully 'set' in your mind-set right now. That will come. The good news is that you can go on with the physical things without having to get the mental things totally in place.

And with that...

RANGE SAFETY, COMBAT SAFETY
The rules are the same. The attitude is different.

The fight is not the range; the range is not the fight.

I have said it before. I will say it again, because it is true. Short of actual wounding and death being allowed and introduced into training, any range activity, however designed and however intensely it is performed, will only get so close to the actual fight any one of us might or will face one day outside of that range. Besides: If wounding and death were a part of it, would it still be training or would it be a fight on the range instead of in the street? So we're back to square one.

Because the range is not the fight, and because we don't normally come very close to getting the 'fight feeling' into range practice, some people question the application, or at least the strict and complete application, of Jeff Cooper's Four Rules Of Firearms Safety to the fight-for-life environment. I know there are people that do that because I used to be one of them. My own questioning of the absolute validity of the Rules under all conditions came to a head following a conversation with what I will call a Four Rules Absolutist (FRA) a few months ago. FRA's are those who, at least in word if not in deed, treat the Colonel Cooper's Rules as…well, absolute in nature and not to be deviated from in the slightest jot or tittle no matter whatever the circumstance or necessity. FRA's are sometimes snickered at by others in the gun world because they don't seem to realize how practically impossible it would be to even own a gun, much less carry and train to fight with it, if the Rules were to be applied as rigidly and absolutely as they imply that they should be. To their credit, most of them realize the practical dichotomies involved and, though still insisting upon rigid adherence where ever possible, they do allow enough leeway in the way the rest of us follow the Rules so that we can still get the work we need to do done.

Still, FRA's can be annoying at times, and this one was, and because of that annoyance I moved my quandaries about the Four Rules as applied to the fight more forward in my consciousness and started thinking harder about it. I mean, really—the organized and controlled range environment where you know most of the time if not all the time what's happening and what's going on versus the chaos and upheaval of sudden violence and the fog of the miniature war that is your response to sudden, unexpected attack by someone trying to kill you and/or others you care about. *Can you seriously expect to apply the Four Rules always and completely to THAT???*

Well, yes, actually. You can. **As long as you remember that the range and the fight are different things.**

To better illustrate that key attitudinal difference, let's examine the Four Rules from both perspectives. I am using the Rules here as they are written in Volume 6, Number 2 of Cooper's Commentaries. He repeats them in other Commentaries and makes comments about them in still others. (Note that there are some who point out inconsistencies and possible contradictions in the various Rule repetitions and comments that he makes about them. These inconsistencies don't bother me, and I hope they don't bother most of you over-much. Colonel Cooper was human like the rest of us are, and we would be apt to do the same things if we wrote and spoke and taught as much as he did. By this time, I certainly hope we all know what he meant to say and do with the Rules.) I will state the Rules under two conditions: Range and Combat. I may phrase the Rule differently for Combat, but I will explain why I'm doing that and hope that you understand the inherent consistency between the two after I'm done.

Let's begin.

Range Safety:

RULE 1 - ALL GUNS ARE ALWAYS LOADED

Note that this is where a lot of people and a lot of posted Rules stop, but it is not the whole of the Rule as Cooper explains it. This is the place where some people will snicker at FRAs because of the apparent inability to handle any firearm if this Rule is to be adhered to with absolute strictness and consistency. Cooper in the same Commentary adds this:

"The only exception to this occurs when one has a weapon in his hands and he has personally unloaded it for checking. As soon as he puts it down, Rule 1 applies again."

In other Commentaries, he uses other words to say in effect that the gun is always loaded until you have verified that it is not. Also, that this applies only so long as the firearm is under your direct control. Put it down, turn away, even for a moment, and you should make the verification check again. This is a solid habit that will help you stay safe.

Combat Safety:

RULE 1 – YOU'D BETTER TREAT THE GUN AS LOADED BECAUSE YOU MADE SURE THAT IT IS LOADED.

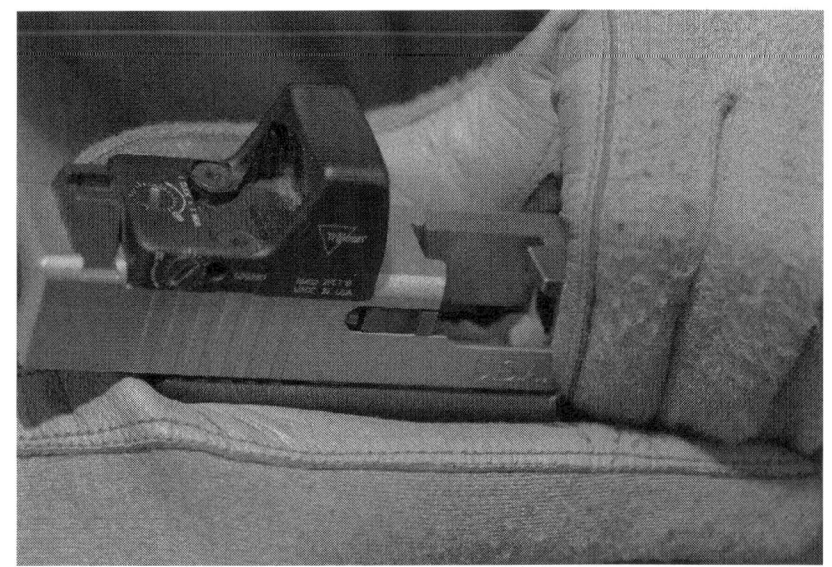

Learn how to do a chamber check and use is wisely and often.

      If you are preparing the weapon for a probable or possible fight for life, you need to make sure that rounds are loaded and that the weapon is ready to fire when and if you need it to. There are stories of police officers who have unknowingly carried unloaded weapons for weeks because they did not make the same kind of verifications that we make on the range and before dry-fire sessions. I'm sure the same forgetfulness has been suffered by others as well. Don't be one of those who forget. Learn the proper way to check your weapon for loaded/unloaded condition, and do so periodically. Whether on the range or in the street, knowing the <u>exact</u> status and condition of any firearm can be the difference between injury and death or health and life.

Range Safety:

RULE 2 - NEVER LET THE MUZZLE COVER ANYTHING YOU ARE NOT PREPARED TO DESTROY.

I sometimes think of it as "If you don't want to see a hole in it, don't point the gun at it." It is clear enough that the Colonel in his writings reinforced it but did not add explanation to it.

Combat Safety:

RULE 2 – GET YOUR MUZZLE ONTO THE TARGET IN THE FASTEST, MOST DIRECT WAY THAT YOU CAN SO THAT, IF NECESSARY, YOU CAN DESTROY IT AS SOON AS POSSIBLE.

The harsh reality as I see it: Somebody starts trying to kill somebody else where you are—whether it's you or another person that's the target at first—it will be next to impossible to avoid muzzle-sweeping yourself or someone else between your holster and the bad guy's center of mass. People will be moving, the bad guy may be moving, shots are coming in (maybe at you, maybe around you, but you can't afford to act like you're not in the way), you'll likely be moving, and sound and fury will signify the chaos that is the life-and-death fight. What I've said before, I'll say again using different words: <u>The safest thing you can do at that moment is to make the bad guy stop</u>. That does not necessarily mean shooting them to the ground. It <u>does</u> mean that you need to be aiming to (in both senses of that word) and ready to and maybe about to when they stop. The way to do that, and to hold the muzzle-sweep of yourself and others to the minimum, is to move the muzzle fast and directly to the point on the attacker that you're going to shoot to.

You do this by perfecting the drawstroke and presentation. You do this by being able to draw the gun from different positions and drive it, quickly and smoothly and under full control, to wherever the target is no matter where it is, and having the gun be set at extension or final position to have the shot on target and nowhere else. You do this by focusing on the goal and not the obstacle, and driving to the goal, to where you want to shoot to. (NOT 'AT'—TO!)

You condition yourself to put the gun on the target, directly on the target, and nowhere else but the target.

No matter the direction, no matter the position you're in when it

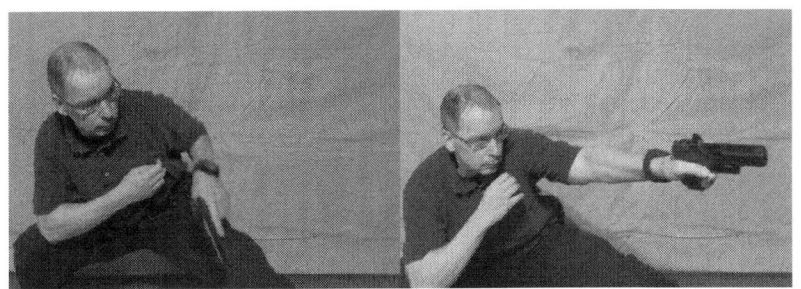

starts, drive the gun to the target...

...only to the target...

...and to nothing but the target. Train yourself to do this.

Realize that this is doing the same thing that Rule 2 says to do. It's just looking at it in a different way. "Don't look at what you're steering away *from*; look at where you're steering *to*." Any of you who drive ever hear that? Any of you who drive ever not heard that? It's the advice I got more than once for how to avoid things that got in front of me on the road. If I looked at the thing I was avoiding, I was more likely to steer to it than around it. Focus on where I want to go, they told me, not on where I don't want to go. I did. It worked. I don't believe the advice is good only for driving and cars, either.

On the range, you will have time and space and the luxury of contemplating what you don't want to do. In the fight, you will have none of that and will have the tunnel-vision focus on the threat besides. Distract yourself with thoughts of avoiding things and you will increase the chance that you go the way you are thinking. Focus on driving to the threat and you are more likely to be able to make things safe again by stopping the threat and being able to put your gun back in the holster, which is as safe a place as it can be if you're carrying it. Focus on what you need and want to do, not on what you don't want to do. Once the focus is there, the mind will direct you around the obstacles and through the gaps you need to get past to reach your goal efficiently, effectively—and safely.

Range Safety:
RULE 3 - KEEP YOUR FINGER OFF THE TRIGGER TIL YOUR SIGHTS ARE ON THE TARGET.

I've also seen and heard this stated as, "Keep your finger off the trigger until you have made a conscious decision to shoot." I will sometimes re-word it this way:

Combat Safety:

RULE 3 – GOT TARGET, GOT THREAT, GOT TRIGGER. NO TARGET, NO THREAT, NO TRIGGER.

The question that either of these forms of Rule 3 poses is: What is a valid target such that your finger goes to the trigger? (I will use target and not threat because you can have a valid threat without having a valid target, but for the civilian mainly and especially, you generally will not have a valid target without a valid threat to go along with it.) Answering that question requires the answers to other questions, and some if not all of the answers to those questions will vary depending on the time, place, and circumstances of the situation. I have seen discussions of what makes someone a valid target go on for many pages of postings on some forums sometimes without consensus being reached. If many minds and some worthy thinkers together cannot provide some hard-and-fast guidelines in pages of dialogue, I'm hard-pressed to think that I can do it in a few paragraphs. I do believe that the more training and (life) experience you have, and the more thought you can put into what qualifies as a valid target ahead of time, the more likely you are to choose correctly at the time you need to decide about it for real.

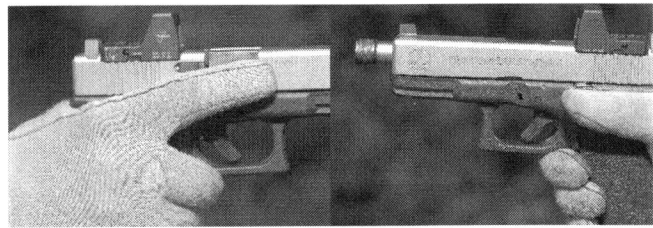

When it is not on the trigger, get the finger up and off the trigger. I prefer and recommend the high index that you see here. Either way, from the other side of the pistol, with proper index you should not see any part of the finger through the trigger guard.

Range Safety:

RULE 4 - BE SURE OF YOUR TARGET.

In another of the Commentaries, Cooper re-phrases the Rule this way:

Identify your target, and what is behind it. Never shoot at anything that you have not positively identified.

I'm not sure if it's a direct quote by the Colonel, but I also see this written as "Be sure of your target and what's beyond (and/or around) it."

Combat Safety:

RULE 4 – BE SURE OF HITTING YOUR TARGET AND NOTHING ELSE. PREPARE SO THAT YOU CAN BE SURE OF HITTING YOUR TARGET, ONLY YOUR TARGET, AND NOTHING BUT YOUR TARGET.

The best place and time in my consideration to program yourself to avoid anything but the target itself is the place where you are and the time before the fight starts. In the same manner that we make surveys of the people and area around us as part of our ongoing practice of awareness, and as we do things like check where the entrances and exits are in an area or building we're in, so we can also consider where the people are and where the areas and things are that we don't want to shoot at or around if a fight does start in that area. By examining the area, the people, and the things that are in that area ahead of time as a habit, we can begin to program our subconscious minds so that they will 'drive' us to the correct spot on the target and away from the incorrect spots anywhere else, and likewise will guide us to the best angles and the best places to fire at and from so as to minimize the chances of a shoot-through. 'Wargame' and 'what-if' ahead of time in the same way that a ring fighter examines the coming fight in their mind or in the way an infantry team rehearses immediate-action drills so that your mind has an idea of where you can move and shoot from with the most safety to everyone else except the bad guy.

Because once the bullets start flying and the knives start cutting (or both), it's likely that you will be 'tunneling in' on the threat. And until the threat is removed, looking at what you're trying to avoid will slow you down and distract you from your efforts to stop the attack and return to a safe condition with the gun back in the holster. Focusing on what you want to do and not on what you don't want to do puts more resources into doing what you want to do quickly and efficiently. Make sure by training and testing and preparation, by thinking and planning and simulation, that you are able to go directly to the threat to end it. Eyes and mind on where you want to go—bad guy stops, no more bullets or blades going anywhere to threaten anybody else—subconscious programmed to direct you there around the other people and other things you don't want and need to shoot so that you don't consciously have to. Gain confidence in your ability to move the gun to the threat and only to the threat so that you can process the rest in the background and avoid things and people without being aware that you're doing so. Be able to hit what you aim at and only that, through the gaps, around the corners, under and over the tables and counters, and without hitting anyone but the bad guy.

You do this through focused training and practice, you do it by planning and plotting and thinking through things in your mind, you do this by knowing where you and your weapon will shoot to under as many conditions from as many positions at as many angles as you can manage to work with. *You become sure of (hitting) your target.*

You prepare and are prepared, in other words to end the fight and win. Quickly. Decisively.

Safely.

Because if you don't win the fight, is anyone going to be safe?

The same Rules applied with a different attitude to attain a single Goal. That's what it's about, isn't it? The Goal?

What is The Goal?

I'll let the Colonel answer that:

"Sometimes it appears we become so obsessed with the ephemeral goal of safety that we lose sight of the purpose of the exercise. *Safety is not first. Safety is second.* **Victory (or success) is first."**

Use the Rules as a path, not an obstacle, to the Goal. That's the way to live.

THE DRAWSTROKE
Is it important to focus on it? If you don't get the gun out, you might die. Is that important to you?

      I wonder sometimes if we, instructors <u>or</u> students, give enough attention to the drawstroke.

      Oh, sure, we practice it endlessly—I hope you do, anyway—but practice is not study, and study is what makes the technique sound when we practice it. And we need a very sound drawstroke, I think, just as soon as we can get it.

      There are two seemingly-obvious questions I need to ask so that you can better understand how important it is to get this down:

      <u>Why, outside of practice and training, would you need to draw the gun to begin with?</u>

Obvious question, obvious answer: You draw the gun because there's a threat to your life or someone else's life *right there, right now*. It's a lethal-force threat, however you and/or the law defines that, and the only way you can stop it is to introduce your own capability to project lethal force if you have to. So, you draw the gun.

So: <u>Given that you are only drawing the gun because you are responding to a right there, right now need to (probably) shoot somebody, what do you need the drawstroke to do?</u>

Think about that a little before you answer.

Why you need a quick, efficient, and consistent drawstroke. You are not normally allowed to have the gun in hand as long as there is no evidence of a lethal-force threat. But if de-escalation fails here and the gun you can't see is revealed, your gun will need to get out and on-target very quickly indeed.

Now that you've thought on it, see if you agree with this:

The drawstroke needs to get you from the holster to on-target shot(s) as quickly and surely as possible.

Think about what that answer does—and does not—cover.

It DOES cover getting the gun—not necessarily the sights, but the gun—on-target.

It DOES cover getting the gun ready to fire as soon as it's clear of the holster, not some time later in the movement.

It DOES cover the need for the right grip, trigger control, and eye\hand coordination.

It DOES cover drawing to any direction, from any position you may be in, whether you are standing still or moving, on demand.

It DOES NOT require you to 'get on the sights' for every single shot no matter what.

It DOES NOT mean you need to end in the same exact position or posture or stance for every shot.

It DOES NOT require you, specifically, to face the target and square up.

It DOES NOT require you to be still when you draw and/or when you shoot.

Some things to consider about the drawstroke:

We hear and read about and see so much of the 'X-count' drawstroke that we may forget that *it's one continuous movement from in-the-holster to ready-to-shoot*. The drawstroke is taught in counts and positions so that the student can learn it more easily and so that each part of the whole movement can be, as needed, examined and practiced and corrected separately. I break it down by steps in my own practice and recommend you do the same. Still, never forget that it's all one continuous movement.

Work for efficiency and quickness before smoothness and speed. Everything should be kept close, movements should be only as large as necessary to get the weapon up and in line to fire, motion from holster to extension/final firing position should be continuous and without pause at any point. If you get efficient, you will most likely look and feel very smooth indeed. It is possible to be very smooth at an inefficient movement, though, so look at efficiency first.

The basic 'X-count' drawstroke. Strive for quickness and efficiency in the movement, train to drive (not <u>punch</u>, <u>drive</u>) the gun directly to the target, and be able to start shooting if necessary as soon as the gun goes level out of the holster.

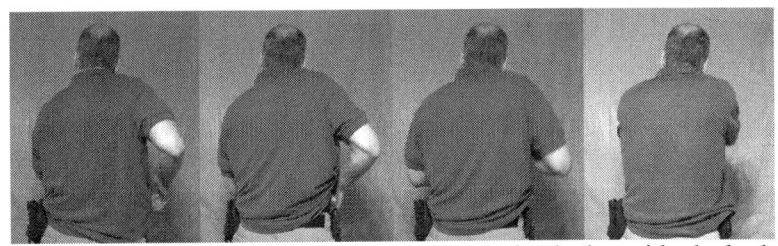

You want your hand and arm to as go straight back alongside the body as possible for best efficiency and least amount of movement. (Some carry positions are easier that others to do this from. Drawing from appendix carry as you see here for example, the elbow moves farther away from the body than I would prefer.) This facilitates the direct presentation of the gun to the target. Unless you have to (back is against a wall, for example), avoid 'chicken winging', which is letting the arm go more sideways that back-and-forth.

No matter what you're doing, no matter where you are, no matter what position you're in: Muzzle straight to target, straight to target, straight to target. Work it until you can do it.

The drawstroke has to set you up to get rounds on target from wherever you are and from whatever position you're in when the fight starts even if you can't 'square up' on the target. How many of you have looked at what it will take to get good shots on someone who's at a 45-degree angle to you when you can't turn toward them? How about 90 degrees? 135? 180? 225? 270? You've got to get the gun 'on' and the eye/hand alignment right even when you don't have the perfect whole-body index to work with.

Speaking of 'drawing to the angles', look at the drawstroke from these two perspectives: Most direct muzzle-to-target plane of draw/line of extension and muzzle-sweep potential. If you're drawing to the side, for example, but the muzzle goes level first and then turns to the target as you extend, you have increased the probability of some problems getting the hits you need and surviving, and you increase the risk that a shot triggered too quickly will not go where you mean it to go. It's not the most efficient way to orient, either. Look at all of that now.

Things that don't change no matter what your position is, where you are or where your target is when the fight starts: Trigger (control), and getting on target (eye/visual center to hand/weapon alignment, whether you're going to sights or not). Make sure this is all consistent no matter where you're drawing from or drawing to, every time.

Some things that will help you to refine your drawstroke are:

Working the parts of the drawstroke in isolation. I do this: I spend a couple of minutes just raising the cover and getting the grip on the gun. Or I work the release from holster and initial rotation. Or the extension, to either one-or-two-hand shooting position, out and back and out and back. I check for a level gun and whether the sights come up in the right spot. I will also check the alternative sighting positions such as metal-on-meat or Type Two Focus. I ask myself: Did I bring the gun up so that it's straight on and straight in for the shot? I check the extension to the angles, looking at how the gun will best rotate to position so the muzzle stays in the target plane. I do these things in isolation as well as put them together.

Overspeed training. One caution: I would not even think about doing this live-fire, at all, period. Overspeed training is basically the performance of an action, in this case the drawstroke, as fast as you possibly can do it. It is a deliberate attempt to run past your normal performance limits. The goal here is pure quickness, a lightning-fast snatch of the gun from the holster into extension or other firing position. It will help you in more ways than just to accelerate your regular draw. Overspeed training has shown me snags in the movement and some problems with where I have put things on my belt, for example.

Record yourself. Until I started doing short demonstration and instructional videos for someone, and now to put on my website, I didn't know that I was 'scooping' on the extension to target. That's just one thing that seeing myself on video has helped me with. All you need is a camera and a tripod and some way to run it back to see what and how you're doing. I would recommend that you don't run video very often. Run the camera, look and see what you need to be working on (or let someone else look at it; sometimes that outside view can be very helpful), work on the inefficiencies and mistakes you have seen for a while, then down the road re-record yourself and check for progress.

And get some training! What…you think I was going to leave that out?

Think about this: Most of the time, we're starting from behind. Even police and military personnel are not allowed to have their guns 'out' and ready to go with as often as they might like to. The rest of us are even more restricted in when and whether we can get the gun in hand before the (physical) fight actually begins. So we're starting from behind. Our drawstroke, combined with things like dynamic movement off the line of first attack, is one of the most important ways we have of getting from behind to even and then to ahead. In cases where our movement is restricted, it may be the *only* way. Because of that, it is important, perhaps vital, to make it as good as we can get it.

Because we may not ever need it, but if the time comes that we do, we will need it to be the best one we've ever made.

NEED FOR SPEED?
Maybe not…or smooth, either, for that matter. And it's not just the drawstroke we're talking about.

As long as we started with the drawstroke...

On one place it was a declarative statement: "Most times, speed of draw is all you need."

In that same place and a another one besides, it was a question: "In reality, how critical is draw speed?"

Then there is the attendant question: "If a fast draw is important, how do I get it?" To which there is a standard attendant answer: "Work to make it smooth. Smooth is fast. Get it smooth and the speed will come."

Well, I've had reason to think about this lately, and I'm no longer convinced that speed is what we should be thinking of, or that striving for a smooth motion is always and absolutely desirable.

I define speed as rate of movement, velocity, distance-over-time, and, important to this discussion, a 'steady-state' situation. You get up to speed and then you maintain that speed. That's how I think about it.

But that's not how a fight, a reactive fight, a fight for life, is going to work, is it? There, it's not accelerate and maintain; it's start-and-stop, change direction, change position, change orientation, here-to-there, zero-to-scary and back to zero, over and over until the fight is done.

It's not a hundred-yard sprint, it's the fastest forty you can manage. It's not the here-to-there of a footrace, it's the ten-yard shuffle drill point-to-point-to-point. It's not the Bonneville Salt Flats with the one-mile measurement after you accelerate, it's the quarter-mile drag race with on-the-edge-of-spinning breakout from the start line and drag chutes at the end.

For the fight, *you don't need speed. The trick is to be quick.*

QUICKNESS. Acceleration and deceleration, from behind, on demand, ALWAYS IN CONTROL. ACCELERATE the gun from the holster, DECELERATE the gun to the shooting position, DIRECT the gun to the target. ACCELERATE off the line of attack, DECELERATE, ACCELERATE to change direction to reset the attacker's Observe-Orient-Decide-Act loop, MOVE yourself as you MOVE the gun, this way, that way, whichever way you need to go to win, ACCEL-DECEL-ACCEL-DECEL. IN CONTROL, ALWAYS IN CONTROL.

When the fight starts, you will not have initiative (usually). You will not have control. Quickness, that zero-to-scary (to the bad guy) controlled/efficient/effective acceleration and deceleration over very short distances and when changing directions, will be what gets the control back for you. Your quick reaction to their action that puts them into reaction and then your quick change of action that keeps them in reaction and again and again and suddenly it's over and they can't act or react and you survived, you prevailed…

…you won…

…but not because you were *fast*. You won because you were *quick*. And it wasn't because you were just quick on the draw. The draw alone isn't enough once the fight starts. You need to be quick, to study and strive for and get controlled and directed quickness, in three areas:

Quick on the draw.

Quick on the move.

Quick on the aim and the trigger when follow-up shots and burst-fire are needed.

The drawstroke first:

The need for the quickest possible presentation comes from the answer to one question: Why are you going to draw the gun?

In most situations, civilians are not allowed to have the gun in their hand much ahead of the very moment when a threat to life is manifest. In other words, you can't draw the gun when you think you might need it, you can only draw the gun when you are convinced that you do need it, whether it is fired at that time or not. In still other words, the gun can only be drawn, most times, only at the near-to-last moment that it has to be in hand and on target.

The attacker/potential attacker does something, you draw. They act, you react. You're starting behind, you need to catch up, and you need to be able to do it quick. You want the gun to go from in the holster under cover (accelerating) to on target (stopped and steady) in the least amount of time possible. In holster/on target; in holster/ready to shoot, without warning and without preparation, in less time than it takes to read the first half of this sentence. Accelerated, decelerated, in control. Steady on the target and in control from any position, even if the potential target is not directly in front of you.

So you need to get quick. How do you get quick? Not by getting smooth. You do it by getting *efficient*.

"*Efficient*: being effective without wasting time or effort; making good, thorough, or careful use of resources; not consuming extra; skillfulness in avoiding wasted time and effort; obtains maximum benefit from a given level of input."

You can be very smooth and destructively inefficient. You can be incredibly smooth with a drawstroke that is too long to save your life. So get efficient first, and add smooth to that after. You train the same way, you practice the same way (slow and easy and making sure of all the motions). It's just a different goal you're working on is all.

I said earlier that you want to be quick and efficient in three areas, of which the drawstroke is only one. Movement and maneuvering is the second area where you need to be quick and efficient to have the best chance of winning. Why? Because unless your drawstroke is supernaturally quick compared to the attacker, or if the gun is already pointed at you, sudden evasive movement is going to give you the best opportunity to keep from getting shot long enough to get your shots on target. Quick and efficient initial evasive movement is what gets the initiative and control away from the attacker and back into your hands. The ability to suddenly change the direction of your evasive movement as you counterattack is what keeps the initiative and control in your hands. Present the attacker(s) an Action that they have to Observe and Orient to before they can Act. Change that action without warning and force them to start processing from the beginning. Continue the sudden and controlled changes until they are stopped by your action or you are able to break contact.

You win; they lose; 'nuff said.

This ability to go from stillness to movement, or normal movement to combat-evasive without warning and to change direction and position quickly is not something most of us can do automatically and on demand. Sports teams and athletes at all levels employ coaches who specialize in nothing but the best ways to move like this and the best ways to teach and train others how to do it. Where I used to teach, instructors examine and adapt concepts from everything from American football to Russian Systema to develop the movement schema that is being passed on to students. Like you study the drawstroke, study movement as well, and in the same way. Get efficient to get quick and smooth it out later. Initially, some separation of these areas, including the third area about to be discussed, will make it easier to train. Do understand, however, that the goal should be, perhaps must be, to combine all of these so that you will be able to go from zero/standing to multiple rounds on target/moving at the very moment it becomes most necessary.

The third area where I believe quickness and efficiency will be of fight-winning value is in the ability to fire accurate bursts and fast follow-up shots. We don't carry pistols because of the fight-stopping power they produce; we carry pistols because we can carry them easily and employ them quickly in close quarters in reaction to sudden assaults. And we don't expect single shots to stop the attack even if they often do. Instead, we anticipate and prepare and train for the necessity to fire repeatedly, quickly, and often. The faster we can put those multiple shots on target, the quicker we can end the fight and the less chance we have of taking damage from the attack we are responding to.

Staying on target with multi-shot strings, bursts of shots, or multi-burst strings, is a matter of attention to fundamentals, particularly recoil management and trigger control. Proper grip to include the correct amount of grip strength to fit the circumstances of the fight (distance/time/need for precision) and experience with riding (not fighting) the recoil of the previous shot gets you back to the consistent index and eye/hand alignment established by the drawstroke and puts you back on either the sights or alternative index you need to fit the situation and get repeated hits in the shortest possible time. Repetitions of the presentation, focusing on eye-sight-hand alignment and index, gets you automatically and quickly back to where you need to be for the next minimum-time shot. Trigger control, to include proper placement, proper and consistent pull of the trigger, and trigger reset gained from focused dry-fire practice and work on precision shooting, trains you to have the trigger ready to go for the next round in the string without pause and without wasted movement or time.

These skills and the ability to fire as if you had a full-auto setting are, I believe, developed by slow repetitions and attention to the details of each component with the goal of making the reset of the weapon between shots efficient and thus quick. Examine and practice the act of firing and shot recovery in the same way you examine and practice the drawstroke, looking first to get efficient in all aspects of grip, alignment and aiming, trigger control, and recoil management. Eventually, this will also be integrated into the drawstroke and presentation and movement and then driven into your subconscious, to be held against the day and the time of greatest need. Done correctly, you will thus be free to make the fighting decisions you need to be making at the time while the gun and the shots, if you need to make them, will, in a way, take care of themselves. *And the fight will be quickly over and you will still be standing.*

That's what's important, isn't it? That you and yours are still standing. That's what's important.

So get quick. To do that, get efficient. All three places and more besides. Get to where you can end it quickly.

Because it's important.

THERE IS NO CONTROVERSY
The argument against point-shooting has been manufactured. Why?

      There is a possibility that someone will read this and think that I've got something against Kelly McCann, who also produced videos and wrote articles and books under the name Jim Grover. They'll be wrong, of course, but because I use excerpts from an otherwise very good presentation he does in Volume 2 of his <u>Inside The Crucible</u> series of videos produced by Paladin Press, they may think that.

      The reality is that I respect the man and his background and experience, I like the way he instructs as it is portrayed on the videos I've seen, and I'm grateful to have had a chance to review this video series. Not only has he presented a lot of really, really good things for me to work on, he has probably solved a point-of-aim/point-of-impact problem I was having during a range session yesterday (at the time of this writing). So even though you're unlikely to ever see this: Thank you, Mr. McCann.

He also showed me how an artificial gap and an either/or illusion can be created if you want to. And make no mistake: The arguments about whether "front-sight-front-sight-front-sight" or the group of aiming techniques that are thrown into the bag labeled "Point Shooting" is best are just as artificial and illusory as they are heated--and they can get very heated indeed.

But...<u>Why</u>? That's the question I ask of both sides, of front-sight-only and of point-shooting-only advocates alike. <u>Why</u> expend effort to make it separate? Why <u>not</u> examine each method and each technique, when and how to use it, how to best perform it, and <u>then</u> teach <u>all</u> of it to people like me just like you do any other technique of shooting and gunfighting? And how is the argument built up and then continued?

Bias, maybe? McCann says: *"I am not a point shooter; never have been....But I also had the government pay me a fair amount of money and give me bazillions of rounds to be sure that that became a normal thing; my arm extended with the front sight was normalcy to me. Most people don't have that luxury; they don't get millions and millions of rounds to do that; I did....But that also kind of jaded me about what people are able to do and what they are not able to do."*

Past training and experience creates an honestly-expressed bias. Hard to fault him or anyone else for it, IF they are expressing honest doubt and asking honest questions and looking for honest proof-of-concept. They have something that is proven and that works for them, perhaps something that has worked for them in a fight, and that has a lot of good history behind it. It doesn't hurt that there is a larger total population of trainers and experienced shooters behind it, either. And, besides, the technique does work. There is no doubt about that.

But...turn it around and look at it from the other side. If those 'bazillions' of rounds had been expended under the guidance of an advocate and trainer of point-shooting techniques, I wouldn't be surprised if that just-as-honestly-expressed bias would have started, "I am not a sighted shooter; never have been...."

It makes me wonder now. If someone like a Jeff Cooper had been around for the government to send Applegate to train with, would we be referring to just the Fairbairn-Sykes method of point-shooting? Or if Fairbairn and Sykes had been helping police in a rural area of China instead of in Shanghai, would the Fairbairn-Applegate-Sykes system include point-shooting or would there mostly be techniques for making longer-range shots with the pistol?

The problem is not bias that is honestly gained and honestly expressed and acknowledged. The problem is a bias that results only from something read or from something heard or limited training and experience. The problem is a bias developed from something taken without thought or question. The problem is how that bias is expressed and whether the biased person is open to new, possibly useful, information even if it threatens the bias. When that happens, a debate that should be helpful to us turns into an argument that is not helpful to anybody including the ones arguing about it.

The problem is when a reasoned debate and a reasoned evaluation of the possibilities and options turns into an unreasoned and unreasoning argument.

Sight alignment--front-sight-press--is one way, as McCann says, to *"place that properly aligned package correctly on your target"*. Various methods that don't emphasize the sights are other ways to place that properly aligned package on your target. Different techniques produce the same result, as long as you put in the time and effort to learn and refine and retain it. McCann says: *"If you're not willing to put in the practice to make sure that happens consistently and under duress, a firearm might not be a good idea for you."* That is as true for point-shooting techniques as it is for sight-shooting techniques.

Bias also occurs because some practitioners don't (apparently) understand or differentiate between a technique (or group of techniques), which could be integrated into their system, and another actual system, which would require a fuller blending and might not work as well with the whole of what they know. There is an important difference between the two that should be understood.

An online dictionary presents this as one definition of *technique*: "The way in which the fundamentals, as of an artistic work, are handled." For this discussion, I'm going to enlarge that just a bit:

Technique, as I will use it, is a simple/basic/limited process or method used to perform a simple or limited-scope task.

A reverse punch is a technique, then, of hitting with the fist. A vertical punch is another technique used to do the same thing: Hit with the fist. Aligning the sights of the pistol, front and back, focusing on the front sight, is a technique used to aim the pistol at the desired target. Aligning the top of the slide of a pistol with the master eye along the straight arm is another technique to do the same thing: aim the pistol at the desired target.

The dictionary defines a *system* as: "A functionally related group of elements" and as "An organized set of interrelated ideas or principles." I use it in the sense of a series or group of techniques (even unto groups of groups or groups of series), logically organized and oriented so as to produce a desired result or goal.

Shotokan Karate is a system designed to help you win a fight. So is Indonesian Silat. What is now called 'Modern Technique' could actually be called the Modern Technique System. It is designed and intended to help you win a fight with guns. So is Massad Ayoob's Stressfire. So is the Applegate method (taken in its entirety). All of these are systems.

Now a lot of the roots of the arguments begin to fall into place in three categories:

1. The sincere belief that your system is the best one, which results in your avocation of it, your defense of it against other systems, and the denigration of competing systems.

2. The 'free market' competition for students, recognition, validation, and income between the various systems.

3. The confusion between a technique or (perhaps more likely) a group of techniques and a system.

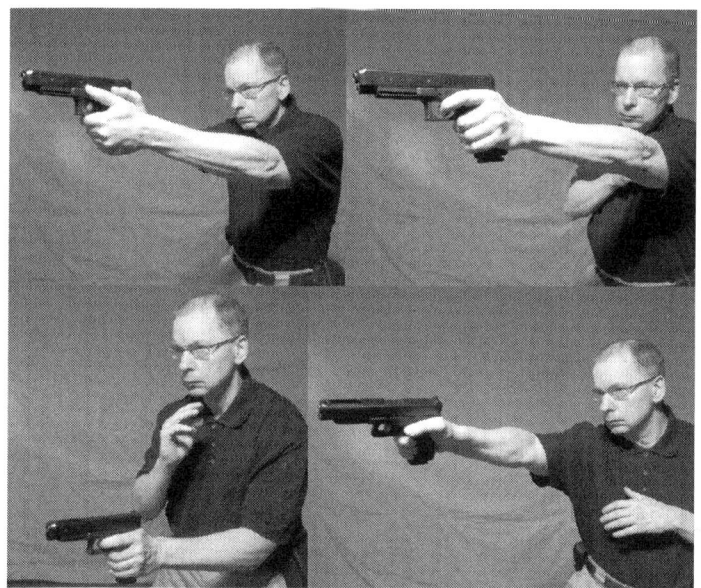

One hand or both hands on the gun, half-hip or point-shoulder, fully on the sights or sighting down the corner of the slide...Why shouldn't it all go together? Why don't more instructors and schools put it all together?

Add ego, add the need to make a living and the wish to make more than a living, add investment of time and money and emotion, add your instructor and your instructor's instructor and their instructors all the way back to Wyatt Earp:

"According to Wyatt Earp, it was an axiom among gunfighters that the man who won a shoot-out was the man who took his time. Shooting at someone who was returning the compliment, Wyatt said, meant, '...going into action with the greatest speed of which a man's muscles are capable, but mentally unflustered by an urge to hurry or the need for complicated nervous and muscular actions which trick shooting involves.'"

Or Wild Bill Hickok:

"I raised my hand to eye level, like pointing a finger, and fired."

Mix with misunderstandings, half-truths, inaccuracy, and inadvertent, even deliberate, hypocrisies, stir it up and bring it to a simmer, and hold there until it's time to serve up one Artificial Argument...

...which leaves us; you and me; the consumers; the students of what we want to be The Art Of Being the One That Goes Home When The Fight Is Over...

Where?

That depends.

On what?

On you and me.

How does it depend on you and me? Like this:

First, consider this statement by Roger Phillips, founder of Fight Focused Concepts: *"Situation dictates tactics; tactics dictate techniques; techniques should not dictate anything."*

Now, consider these ideas:

Sights-only shooting has gotten a lot of people home after the fight.

Point-shooting has gotten a lot of people home after the fight.

<u>However:</u> Though each technique and system can be stretched to cover the areas that the other system is best at, it still is a fact that each technique and system is strong in some areas and weak at covering others.

<u>Which means that:</u> The system most likely to get us home after the fight is going to be one that uses techniques of both sighted and point-shooting, and that trains us to have the judgment and

ability to employ whatever technique best covers the situation we find ourselves in, no matter what that situation is.

Kelly McCann (as Jim Grover), demonstrating very-short-range shooting techniques in his Combative Pistol video, makes almost the same point: *"(Someone at a conference he attended, asking)...which would you prefer? Would you prefer that someone discounts it and never does it and then finds themselves having to do it, and never practiced, or be familiar with it and at least be proficient so if it ever does occur, he can do it? Made a lot of sense to me."*

THEREFORE: We, the consumers, should do our best to seek out and pay for training from instructors who have successfully integrated techniques and systems and who can teach us to do the same on an as-needed basis.

There are such instructors, though they appear at this time to still be in the minority. They don't seem to be as hard to find and get to as monks on the mountaintop, but it may take some investigation and interrogation to find them. Wherever they are found, they should be encouraged with our business. Others, those who want to force us into one mold, one side or the other of this argument, should be encouraged to change their thinking by the drop-off in business that their adherence to old misconceptions and rigid thinking brings to them.

Seek the best. Avoid the workable-but-not-quite-as-good. And don't let yourself get caught up in this manufactured conflict.

Because, really: Would you rather be choosing sides in an argument that doesn't have to be?

Or getting the best chance you can to be able to go home after the fight is over?

Think before you answer those questions. Your life may depend on it.

WHAT THEY'RE NOT TELLING YOU ABOUT POINT SHOOTING
Ever wondered what some 'experts' on both sides of the alternative-aiming argument don't want you to be thinking about? I have some ideas about that...

In the previous section I explained how the ongoing arguments between both sides of the alternative-aiming aisle had been created in some ways, how it was not only artificial in many respects but just not practical and useful to continue any more, and that there really was no controversial aspect to the learning and use of both full-on-sights shooting and point-shooting in all their aspects and variants.

The arguments continue and the controversy continues, however. I have watched videos and read comments that make various specious claims about, mostly, point-shooting, and I've come across a statement or two about sights-on shooting as well. I will address both sides here. Understand, however, that since the overwhelming amount of argument is against alternative-aiming methodologies, most of what I offer in considered speculation will be about that.

Here is my suspicion: Not everyone who makes videos and writes articles where they espouse at length about how point-shooting doesn't work believes what they're saying about it. There are some that actually do, no doubt--as unbelievable as that is--but it's hard for me to think that they are anything but an unthinking and near-mindless minority of the 'contra-pointing' population.

If, as I suspect, they don't believe what they are saying, two questions suggest themselves to me:

What are they _not_ telling us?

Why are they not telling us?

Here's what I think a generic contra-point-shooting instructor is not telling you:

I know it works and I know it has a proven history of saving lives in war and on the street.

From before Wild Bill Hickok wrote in a letter about how he, "raised my hand to eye level, like pointing a finger, and fired," to Applegate's OSS trainees using Fairbairn's 'Shooting To Live' techniques in Europe, to a man who sold me a gun a couple of years ago who recently put 7 of 7 Speer Gold Dot rounds out of a Walther P-99 into a man that pointed a .38 at him in Colombia just a few weeks ago, point shooting has been saving lives, winning gunfights, and dropping bad guys. Anyone who has looked at all at point shooting is going to see this pretty quickly.

I know it is the most useful single shooting skill for most people under average gunfight conditions.

All you have to do to figure that out is to look at the situations, conditions, and circumstances under which the majority of self-defensive shootings take place and then look at the average amount of experience and practice and training with a handgun that most people in those situations have. Sight-on techniques are useful and used, yes, but the majority of situations seen favor a point-shooting solution.

I know that it is easy to teach someone to a level of 'combat competency' pretty quickly and faster than using all-sights-shooting techniques.

It's not instantaneous, not as fast as some might say, but a basic level of ability to get rounds on target at what are still average confrontation distances can be obtained demonstrably faster by teaching point-shooting than by working only on front-sight-press-front-sight-press and repeat.

I know that point-shooting skills are retained longer than sighted-shooting skills, that they can be kept up more easily, and that they don't degrade as much or as quickly without practice.

I can't tell you exactly why; I suspect it's because more of sighted shooting technique as it is taught by some is contrary to the way the body wants to work under threat than is the corresponding point shooting technique. Point-shooting skills, while still needing to be trained, are yet more 'natural' to the shooter than are sight-shooting skills. Thus they are learned more quickly and easily and forgotten by the body and the mind more slowly. So you don't lose as much over time and it's easier to get it back when you start practicing again.

I can't or don't know how to teach you an integrated system that meets your needs and gives you the best chance of survival and victory in a gunfight.

So they try to convince you, and maybe themselves, that the part they have is the only part you'll ever need, or that the part they have is the whole of what's needed. It's surprising how long some of them have succeeded in doing that.

There may be more things they're not saying, but those are the more common and important things that are left out of the monologues. But it's not just the anti-point-shooters that leave things out. There's at least a couple of things that some pro-point-shooters leave out of their monologues, such as:

I know that point-shooting techniques aren't the best thing for every shooting situation or need.

Believe it or not, there are a couple, at least, out there that want you to believe that point shooting methods can be the be-all and end-all of defensive handgun needs, covering every condition, every range, every situation, every kind of encounter.   Or at least all but a very, very unlikely few. To put the rebuttal simply: They're not, they won't.

Dove-tailing with that excluded statement is:

I know that you should be on the sights whenever you can be, even at closer ranges where point-shooting works really well.

The better you can shoot, given the time and circumstances you will need to shoot (response to a lethal-force assault), the better you should shoot, and sights are better when you have the time and ability to go to them. That's why the progressive instructors, even those that teach only or mostly point shooting methods, will tell you that sights are preferred. They recognize that you can't always get on them all the way, but when you can, they will say that's what you should do. Going to sights should be the default, point-shooting should be the fallback position in most cases. Not all, but most.

So that's what I think is what is not, sometimes, being said. The question that follows is "*Why are they not saying it?*"

My belief? Money, Ego, Power. It's mostly if not completely one of those aspects or some combination of them, I think. Which of the three it is in a given case depends on a number of factors such as the personality of the instructor in question, their financial strength (their ability to afford being an instructor and/or run a school, in other words), and their perceived 'place' in the industry. Simply put, if a given instructor can't or won't teach point shooting, it is in their interest to convince the customer base—us—that we don't need to learn it. If they can't do that--if we see the usefulness of the system and the need to have a fully-integrated set of skills that cover the largest number of situations where someone is trying to kill us--then we will take our money, our attention, and our loyalty and give it to someone who can teach us what they can't or won't. This process is also known as the Free Market. Without all the information, though, we won't be able to make the right buying decisions that give us the best chance of being on our feet when the last shot is fired. The longer our hypothetical instructor can keep enough information away from us about this, the longer we will give them whatever they want and need from us.

(Note that I don't have any problem whatsoever with making money. What I have a problem with is making money by or while you short-change the customer, especially where training that can mean the difference between life or death for that customer is concerned.)

The question that may come up is: "You mean to say they don't really care about _me_ and about doing the best thing for _me_?"

I considered that for a while and finally asked myself this question: "If they, those who deliberately leave out things, really _did_ care about the people they teach, why aren't they including and integrating point shooting techniques and concepts into their training, their systems, and their methodologies? Or vice-versa, where sighted shooting is left out and the sole and total emphasis is on point-shooting systems?"

The answer that comes up is: Maybe they _don't_ care. Or at least, not as much as they say they do. Or, they care more about something else (making money easier, undercutting others and/or rising in their perceived pecking order in the industry, shielding their egos, things like that) than they do about presenting the full and complete package to their students.

That's a hard answer that I don't like making. But it seems too logical an answer to not make it.

So, what do you do if it is or becomes evident that a given instructor or school is leaving things out? The simple answer is the same one I provided in the previous section: Take your time, your attention, and your money, find an instructor that puts everything important together, that doesn't leave anything out, that gives you what you need and not what they want, and invest in them. Find someone that will return full and complete value not just for the treasure you invest with them, but for the trust you place in them to help you learn how to keep you and yours alive.

Do that and you will get a return that you can depend on, and you will not regret the effort you make to get it.

ANOTHER DEFINITION OF POINT SHOOTING

The usual definition is that it's pointing the gun at the target and shooting without using the normal sights. It occurs to me that it **could also be defined as methods of shooting to a point**. We always hear, "Aim small to miss small", right?

Roger Phillips keeps telling us to focus on a specific place, a specific point if you will, and there the shot should go. Shooting points is point-shooting. Like hunting deer is also deer-hunting.

A small thought, but an interesting one to me.

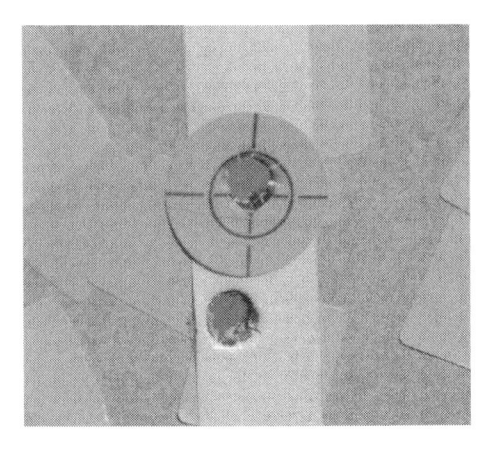

Accuracy is King--but Monarchs do Fall
Terminal effect is Queen, and she has a power all her own. Pay attention to her.

It comes up almost every time, if not every single time, a discussion of terminal effect or debate between various calibers comes up: Someone will always throw in a variation of the "If you're accurate, it doesn't matter what you're shooting." argument. This argument reached its epitome in my experience on an Internet gun forum where I read this statement:

"Accuracy rules and will always top out **any and ALL** choices of ammo."

But that's not true, is it? Not as absolutely stated as it is, it's not. If accuracy really and truly trumped all other considerations, we could ditch the 9s and the 40s and everything else and all start carrying .22s for self-defense. Because I can get accurate faster and shoot more accurately with a .22 than with anything else I currently carry.

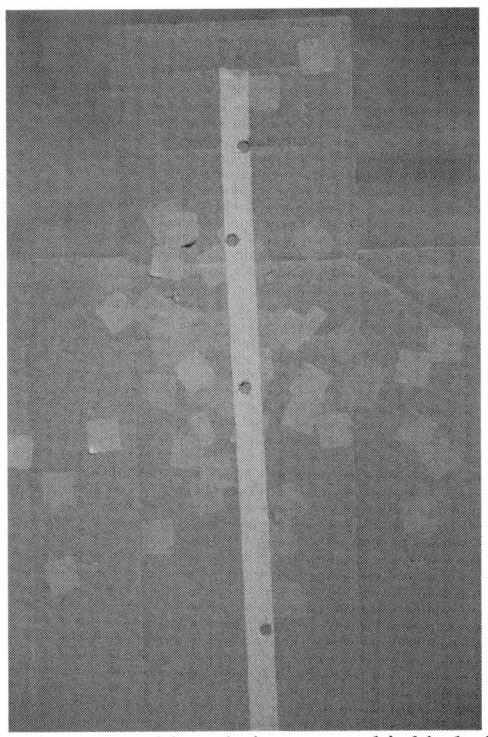

Without effective ammunition choices, even this kind of placement will fail to stop the attack.

But nobody has done that (if they don't have to; some simply are unable to shoot anything bigger), have they? Because we can't, if we want the best chance of winning the fight. We can't carry .22s because .22s, as lethal as they are (and they <u>are</u> lethal; lots of people die after being shot with .22s every year), don't give us everything we need. Because we don't just need lethality, we need <u>fight-stopping effect</u>.

That means we need to pay attention to terminal effect, and that means we need to pay attention to the ammunition we put in our carry guns, and we need to consider the usefulness of accurate burst-fire. Even the best handgun ammunition cannot be relied on as a single-shot fight-stopper, though it often does exactly that. And if we

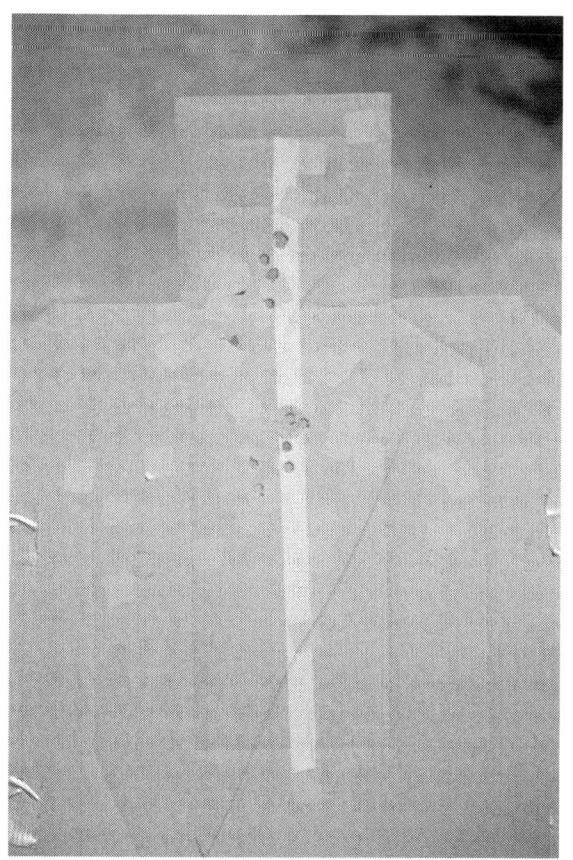

We don't carry handguns because they're powerful but because they're easy to carry. Accurate burst-fire is one of the best ways to compensate for the weakness of even the best-designed handgun rounds.

do not have the best handgun ammunition in the gun, then accurate burst-fire is the most practical way to make up for the lack of terminal performance of the rounds we do have. And accurate burst-fire is the most practical way also to reduce the chances that even the premium and proven rounds will fail, as we know they do sometimes.

This does complicate the choice of handgun and ammunition combination somewhat, but it is a necessary complication. We need to choose and use a handgun that we can hit with well with bursts of rounds, not just single shots. Then we need to find the best ammunition we can find to fire those bursts out of that handgun with.

Don't get me wrong: **Accuracy is still King. But if Accuracy is King, then Terminal Effect is Queen and her rulings must also be attended to**. If we are to make the best choice of equipment to give ourselves the best chance of going home after the fight is over, BOTH must be considered, developed, and chosen as best we can.

Our lives depend on it.

CARRYING WITHOUT A ROUND CHAMBERED
Can you? Sure. Do you want to? Probably not. Here's why:

I see this question asked on gun-forums periodically:

Is it advisable to carry a handgun (for self-defense) without a round in the chamber?

There is also a related question that is sometimes asked:

Is it really safe to carry a handgun (for self-defense) without a round in the chamber?

The base answers, in short, are: NO and Yes (in one sense) and No (in another).

Here's the expansion on that:

Please consider what you carry the pistol for, and what you will need to do with it. That is, the civilian carries a pistol because they don't know when an attack will come and they need something close to hand that can be employed with near-zero to zero warning. (Of the start of the attack, that is. You may have some sign/warning that an attack probably or certainly is coming, but you still don't always know exactly <u>when</u> it will happen.) That means it has to be ready <u>right then</u>; it has to be able to fire <u>right then</u>. When an attacker is reaching for a gun or has one on you already, any delay is unacceptable; when an attacker is running at you with a knife in their hand, any delay is unacceptable. When you're under threat of death or grave bodily harm, any delay is unacceptable.

Let me put it another way.

IN THE TIME IT TAKES YOU TO DRAW THE PISTOL AND CHAMBER A ROUND YOU COULD DIE.

It's that simple. Not having a round available <u>right then</u> could get you killed. Therefore, it is best to carry with a round chambered.

"But you haven't seen how fast I can rack the slide," some will say, "I practice that constantly and can get the pistol into action very fast."

Well and good. So can the Israelis, who teach some pistol techniques that integrate the chambering process into the presentation. They can and do perform it remarkably quickly.

You should not. You should carry a modern-design pistol in a good holster with a round in the chamber.

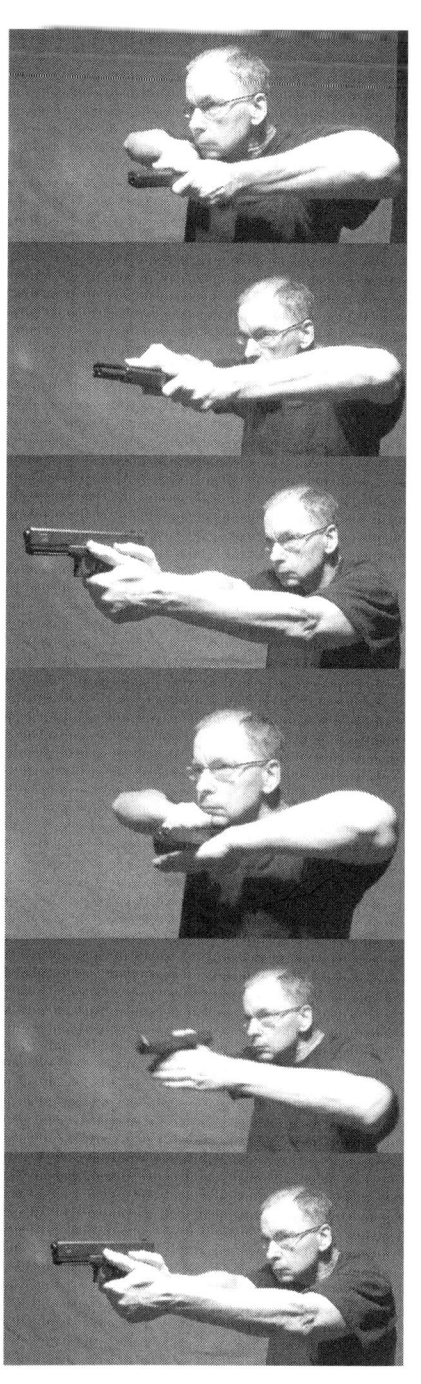

What some people apparently don't know is that the Israeli method of shooting does not require you to carry unchambered. Author illustrates the method incorporating a chamber (top three) as it is most often seen and then repeating the technique (bottom three) as if a round is already in chamber.

Even in Israel, none of their first-tier military units carry a handgun unchambered and in the general population unchambered carry is becoming less common as a carry option.

Here's how to prove it:

Take the following three tests. If you can, do the first two with an Airsoft replica pistol that operates like your carry pistol or at least a modern firearm, and an opponent with a rubber/practice knife. The last test can be, and probably should be, taken with your actual carry weapon. <u>All tests are to be done with the pistol set up as it is for normal, everyday carry</u>. (In most places and cases, that means under cover and in the normal concealment holster. Don't lie to yourself by using range-only gear in this case. It's too important a subject to allow yourself that crutch.)

1. "Attacker" with knife starts not more than 25 feet away from you, and will initiate the test by charging at you with the knife. Draw, chamber, and fire at least one, preferably two, disabling shots before they can hit you with the knife. You are allowed to dodge, retreat, or otherwise move around as you do this.

2. "Attacker" with knife starts not more than six feet away, and initiates the test by attacking. You must avoid a crippling or killing cut or thrust in any way you see fit, but must end the attack by drawing, chambering, and firing your pistol, scoring at least one good hit.

3. Put what is normally your support hand in a sling. (If you don't have a sling, grab your belt or tuck it in your waistband or immobilize it somehow.) At the signal, draw, chamber, and fire one round without using the immobilized hand in any way.

Above: Not the best time or place to be trying to chamber a round. Below: Sure, you can rack with one hand if needed. But if the pistol is already in your hand, what would you rather be doing? Racking it, or shooting him with it?

    If you successfully avoid major damage in the attack tests and can operate the pistol one-handed in test three, then you are better than I am and I wish you well. (I can draw and chamber and fire a round one-handed from concealment, but you may can do it faster.) You may indeed be okay without a round in the chamber. I don't really think so, but maybe you will be. I still think you should have one ready, though.

As for the Israeli method I mentioned earlier, there are specific reasons the Israelis originally developed that particular operating technique. The reasons and circumstances for that are not the same as they are here. Therefore, it does not seem appropriate to copy their methods. Besides that, Israeli civilian trainers are moving away from the empty-chamber carry idea, and Israeli military and police specialty and special-operations units do not carry their sidearms unchambered. If those who train longest and hardest for violence they know they will encounter don't think it best to go empty-chambered, why should you?

The second question is, is it safe? The answer is, mostly yes. I say "mostly" because there are circumstances that could present a hazard--usually, some older pistol designs (those that don't incorporate the multiple internal safeties that modern pistols do), some simply-old pistols or heavily-used pistols (materials and mechanisms wear out and down and break, even in the best-made mechanisms), and when the pistol is carried in an unsafe way (stuck in the belt or a pocket without a holster or some way to cover the trigger, for example).

In general, though, modern designs incorporate a number of mechanisms both inside and outside which have the sole purpose of keeping the hammer or striker away from the firing pin until <u>you</u> decide you want them to meet.

You can demonstrate that to yourself with this exercise: Unload the weapon, check that you've unloaded the weapon, and then check that there isn't any live ammunition in the weapon. (Make this both a visual and tactile check. Have someone else confirm the unloaded condition if you can.) Then, rack the slide to engage the hammer or striker. If the pistol has external safeties, set them and put the weapon in your normal holster wherever you intend to carry it on your body. If there are no external safeties, just holster the weapon.

Now, do something physical. Work around the house, bend and twist, stretch and lift, run and jump, do yoga or Pilates, whatever-

-just move around. If you want, you can even hit yourself around and on the holster as a further test. My bet is that the gun won't trigger, you won't hear the "click" of the hammer falling, and that when you're ready you will be able to remove the weapon from the holster, point it in a safe direction, pull the trigger, and hear the "click". And that will only happen when you are ready for it, and not before.

(I also recognize that no production of man is perfect or without error in all instances. So if you perform this test and <u>do</u> at some point hear the hammer fall, or see that the pistol has triggered itself without you pulling the trigger, then check your placement and trigger cover and repeat the test, preferably twice more. If you get another "click", get the gun to the manufacturer for immediate repair or replacement!!)

So: A modern-design pistol in good condition, a proper holster that covers the trigger until the pistol is drawn and the engagement of the <u>most important safety of all--the one between your ears</u>--and you will be as safe with your pistol as the many, many thousands of people have been that carry every day with a chambered round in a pistol that is ready to go when they need it to and not an instant later.

I hope this helps.

RESISTING A HOME INVASION I: IMMEDIATE ACTION DRILLS

It always shows up at a certain stage of firearms training and it often shows up on DVDs and in books that present tactics and techniques and strategy:

House Clearing--pieing corners, approaching doorways and intersections, using flashlights, shooting at close ranges, how to set up and use a 'safe room', things like that. Go just a bit beyond basic defensive gunfighting, and you will find a lot of suggestions about how to deal with that 'bump in the night' that you hope you never hear.

But what if the first sign of an intrusion is not a bump, but a crash, the sound of the front door giving way to the impact of a foot or a body? And what if the safe room is on the opposite side of the two to four men that is the average reported home invasion?

In December of 2008, Gabe Suarez published an article about home defense (Street Tactics: Fighting in Your House) in Concealed Carry Magazine. In that article, he identified four 'missions' that a civilian defender might undertake in defense of home and family: *Holding Ground, Taking Ground, Traversing Through,* and *Search And Clear.* Given increasing reports of violent home invasions that have occurred since then, I suggest another category: *Immediate Action Drills.*

"Immediate Action Drills are drills designed to provide swift and positive reaction to sudden violence." – modified from Combat Training of the Individual Soldier and Patrolling, July 1967.
IADs are simple plans that can be 'pre-programmed' to start under certain conditions without you having to think about what to do. Tap-Rack-Assess is an example of an IAD. An IAD as I define it will be something that you do without thinking to get you to a point where you can start thinking in whatever way the fight allows for. An IAD is not a complete plan; it is a 'catch-up', something that gets you from behind to at least even if not ahead as near to instantly as possible.

It Starts Where You Live

If you're in your house, stop reading and look around at where you are. Not like any shoot-house you've ever seen or been in, I'd bet. Make a sweep, look at what and who is in the room: furniture, stuff on the floor, pets, Significant Other, kids. Where's the nearest outside door? How does the access to and from the rest of the house look from where you are now?

You've trained in this hallway...What about in this one?

You've trained in this room...Have you trained in this one?

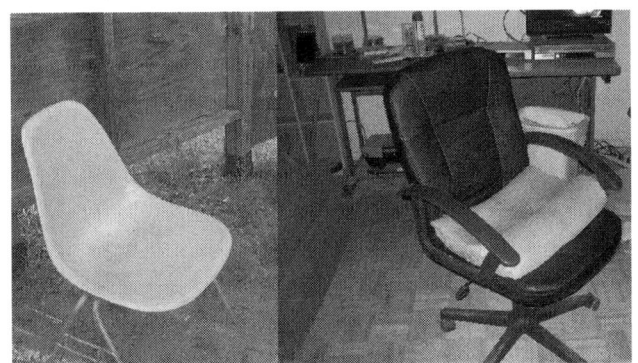

You've practiced draws from this chair...Have you practiced draws out of this one?

    Now take a few seconds and imagine (usually) men, armed men, forcing their way in through the front or side or back doors and into your house. <u>Fight's on</u>. (Unless you want to depend on them getting what they want and then leaving you unharmed?....I didn't think so....) SO and children are running and/or screaming or standing in terrified shock, dogs are barking, maybe attacking, maybe cringing, cats are running to hiding places, stuff is falling and breaking, there is shouting, maybe shooting already, and you are...

Thinking that it's not like any house-clearing exercise you've ever done, I'd bet.

You've got a mental sketch of the problem now. Let's look at some ways to deal with it.

Can you draw from here (the chair) to there (the doorway)? Without standing? If your safe room is back that way and you need to clear the path to it, can you do that?

Prevention and Delay

There are a lot of guides about how to harden your home to prevent intrusion. Against the home invasion specifically, look at two: ways to see outside without opening a door, and hardening both the door and the door-frame area.

Many home invasions begin with an innocent presentation – someone knocks and asks for help, hoping you will open up and let them in to kill you. To help prevent the 'scam' entry I suggest a system of cameras, mirrors, peepholes, anything that gives you a clear view of at least the doorway area and a few yards beyond. You need to be able to see who is in front of the door, who is behind and beside them, and who is a few yards away looking like they're waiting for their partner(s) to make the opening they need. Ideally, the system should have some night-vision capability so that you don't have to depend on the lights working for your threat assessment. The vision system does not have to be expensive or elaborate to do the job.

When considering hardening the door, pay special attention to the door-frame and attachments. Against a physical assault, the latches and hinges are more likely to give way before the door itself breaks as long as you start with a good solid door. So make sure the frame is thick and strong and the screws and latches are strong and deep where they go into the frame.

The purpose of the vision system is to prevent the easy entry of a home invader and to warn you of a developing attack. The purpose of the hardened door is to warn you of a sudden attack and to delay the intrusion long enough for you to get your reaction plan started.

Speaking of reaction plans...

THE GOAL IS TO WIN. I define winning as you and yours being alive and unharmed and the attackers either dead, surrendering, or running away when the fight is over. There are three ways to reach this goal:

1. Fight—defeat or destroy them.
2. Escape—get everybody away from them.
3. Bunker up—reach a solid defensive position and hold them off until help arrives.

The strategy you chose will depend on the way your specific fight develops at the time as much as on what you have planned ahead of that time. One thing to keep in mind is that you're almost certainly going to have to fight no matter which option you take. Not only that, but the last two options will likely force you into perhaps the most difficult kind of fight you can have, a fighting retreat under violent pressure.

Not very much like the normal house-clearing exercise, I bet.

So, where is your gun?

If you can't bring it to bear within the first couple of seconds of an intrusion (obviously, the faster the better), you are going to be in a difficult position.

"You mean I can't leave the gun in the bedroom when I'm home?"

Not if you want to be able to bring the gun to bear quickly against a sudden intrusion from wherever you are in the house. In the case of a home invasion, I believe that the first seconds will be critical to your survival. Whatever response option you choose at that moment, the ability to put fire on the threat immediately could easily make or break your response strategy and the ultimate outcome of the fight. However you do it, where ever you put it, you need to be able to get to the gun <u>fast</u>.

An excellent rifle and more powerful than a pistol, but useless to me if I have to deal with someone right then and right where I am.

"Not a problem; I wear the gun in the house and I can draw to first shot in a second and a half, usually less."

That's fine; can you do it sitting down? Leaning back in the Laz-E-Boy? From the office chair you sit at your computer desk with? (You know, the one with the arms.) The way you're normally dressed at home? Are you sure? Have you practiced it?   Until you have, how can you be sure?

If you have a long gun somewhere ready to go, have you even walked through the route and practiced accessing it quickly? If you're able, have you ever set it up at the distance and with the zigs and zags you would have to take in your house and run a live-fire 'run, grab, and gun' exercise?

And can you fight your way to not just a rifle, but any gun you have? Even the one you're wearing? If the attack develops quickly enough or if you're close to where the attackers enter, going directly for the gun may be the wrong initial answer. You need some simple combatives skills to give you time and space and to disrupt the contact-range attack enough to get the weapon into play with the least risk to you and yours. As it is dangerous to 'think gun' without exception on the street, it is dangerous to focus solely on the hammer even when the problem in your home is not a nail.

You have to 'Out-Violence' them

I can't take credit for that term; I can only tell you that it makes sense. Let's be honest: Even if you have a few seconds warning, you will likely find yourself on the wrong end of the initiative curve at first. The invaders have a plan and will execute it with confidence usually born of previous success. You will have your plan and the shocked realization that you need to go NOWNOWNOW if you and your family are going to survive longer than about thirty more seconds.

To do that and win, I believe you need to do three things for at least three seconds, maybe longer: Be automatic. Go very hard. Get very violent.

Most criminals act with the expectation that the victim will cooperate with them to some extent. The sooner you can show them something they are not expecting, the more likely it is that they will be shocked and confused enough to let you take their initiative for yourself. Your first automatic (semi-automatic, actually; there will have to be some thought involved so you can adapt, but it has to be minimal) reaction must be designed to do that.

Can you be 18 again for thirty seconds? That's what 'go very hard' means. Not many of us can be like we were in high school for very long, but I believe that most healthy adults can condition themselves to go that hard and nearly that fast for that long in an emergency. Some, for various reasons, cannot, but if you are otherwise healthy and cannot, now is the time to begin the conditioning program to let you do that. It's not just a home invasion emergency you will be helping yourself to cope with; there are a lot of situations where a short burst of strength and speed will get you home again when it's over.

Going very hard will help you get very violent, the last component of the initial defensive reaction. Whether it is the smashing, ripping and tearing, gouging and pounding techniques of military combatives, picking up a chair and trying to crush their skull, grabbing a kitchen knife and driving it through their heart, or the more refined technique of emptying a magazine into them so fast they think you have an automatic weapon in hand, the aim is the same: To produce a few seconds of massive counter-violence that allows you to win, however you define it at the time.

Because if you can't win, what else is going to matter?

That's the concept, then. A different one than you may be used to, but not unattainable with a bit of thought and some preparation beforehand. I'm one of a number of people who wish we didn't have to think about this, but the reports are coming in, and they say that wishes don't matter. Like it or not, the unthinkable must be thought upon.

Here's hoping you never have to do more than think about it.

RESISTING A HOME INVASION II: TOOLS, TACTICS, TECHNIQUES

      In the previous chapter I laid out what I believe to be some concepts that would be useful in planning your response to a violent home invasion. Now it's time to get more specific about what you use to apply those concepts and how you use it.

      Before I continue, I want to make sure you are reminded and understand: The previous chapter and this one you are reading now deal only with the immediate response to a violent invasion of your home. They are not intended and not meant to suggest responses to bumps in the night or situations where the nature of the intrusion is unknown in some respect. The concepts suggested here are <u>only</u> meant to cover an immediate assault on you and your family in your home. Please be clear on this point.

That said:

What is the core problem beyond the actual attack?

Since we're talking tools and techniques, the core problem is reach, length, and space. Whatever you use and however you decide to do it, you have to consider the space you will be doing it in. That's defined not only by the size of the rooms and hallways, but also by what's inside those rooms and hallways, the size (mainly length) of the weapons you are using, and the need to go through openings and around corners. The terrain you are and will be fighting on and over is the key here. Tools and tactics have to accommodate both the terrain and the actions of the invader(s).

One of the central questions you need to make sure you answer-- maneuvering space. Shown in a typical hallway: (Here) Sig 556R; AR with stock in normal firing position and fully collapsed; Beretta CX4 Storm; (Next page) Tavor bullpup; AR pistol; G19 (using close-in grip).

On the surface, it looks as if the pistol is the ideal choice for maneuvering through the home. Other factors might make a rifle a better choice, however. Let the situation dictate the tools, not the tools the situation, as much as possible.

Handgun, Rifle, or Shotgun? What's best?

That depends...

For Immediate/Initial Response: Handgun. Why? It's most likely to be on you or in reach, it can be brought into action faster than a long-gun, even one that's beside you when the door caves in, and it is easier to keep in possession and in action in the close-range fight that will occur in the first moments of violence.

For Bunkering Up: The rifle by a small margin. A shotgun will hit harder on a per-round basis, but magazine capacity is limited on most. And buckshot will not spread enough to give you much of a chance of hitting more than one bad guy at a time. (Pattern the shot at hall-length range and see. You should do that with a defensive shotgun anyway.) A rifle offers the possibility of higher magazine capacity, precision-shot capability, and handles easier than the shotgun (usually). Planning for a worst-case problem where they don't go away after a shot or two is fired (yes, that's likely, but planning for 'likely' can get you killed very dead), the rifle offers more flexibility and better *combat power* (not the same as *firepower*) than the shotgun. The shotgun is second choice for this.

For Movement and Maneuver: Trickier, but first choice goes back to the handgun. It offers more flexibility and is easier to control and move around with, especially in the dark and when you need a hand for something (flashlight) or someone (guiding someone else). It also is easier to defend if you get surprised at close range while moving. Second choice goes to the carbine. The extra two inches of length add more difficulty to moving with the shotgun inside the house than you might think, and since you likely won't have reloads with you, the additional ammunition capacity of the carbine could be very comforting.

In states that allow it (check your state's laws), consider an SBS or SBR (short-barreled shotgun or rifle) for a dedicated home-defense weapon. It requires registration with ATF and the one-time tax, plus cost of modifications. But the reduction in length and weight, if you have to move with it, could be a real advantage in an indoor fight for life. It will be much handier with a suppressor attached, said suppressor being strongly suggested for a dedicated in-house gun if you live in an area that allows you to have one.

A note about caliber and ammunition: I favor rifles over shotguns, and smaller calibers over larger for those rifles where home defense specifically is concerned. For this reason I think that the PCC (Pistol Caliber Carbine) should be a serious consideration, especially if the carbine in question is dedicated or primarily to be used indoors/in-house. (There is a reason why the favored weapon among police entry teams was for a very long time the H&K MP5 submachine gun seldom, if ever, employed with a full-auto setting.)

Consider the Pistol Caliber Carbine as a dedicated or primary-use weapon for indoor and other short-range applications.

Among the pluses a PCC offers is lower recoil, less muzzle flash, and lower volume when fired (Still very loud, as anything will be indoors, but not as bad as a rifle.) and more precision than the handgun. It could also provide economies by using the same ammunition as you use in the pistol, as well as being easier for smaller/younger members of the family to shoot with.

In the 'real' rifle category, I lean to the 5.56 x 45/.223 or 5.45 x 39 as a preference unless you have a lot of empty space around your house. These calibers also are easier for smaller/younger family members to manage, and both are common. The 5.56/.223 round in particular has a lot of variations available, including some designed primarily for use inside buildings. There are fewer choices in 5.45, though as of the time of this writing Hornady has started the US-production-ball rolling with a V-Max variant in this caliber that looks like a good choice.

If you choose to or have to run a heavier caliber--7.62 x 39 or 7.62 x 51/.308, one of the popular hunting calibers, or much else larger than what the AR or AK-74 model rifles use--it would be advisable to give a lot of thought to what ammunition you load into that rifle if you plan to use it inside your home. Consider frangible or pre-fragmented rounds, lightweight softpoint ammunition, or more purpose-designed rounds such as the TAP round made by Hornady or the MPG round made by Corbon.

If you're going to run an MBR (Main Battle Rifle) such as this FAL for home defense, give hard consideration to the ammunition you load into it.

Where pistol rounds are concerned, it depends on whether the pistol is going to be dedicated to home defense or carried outside as well. If the former, something like a frangible or pre-fragmented round such as the Glaser or Critical Defense is a consideration, though not as serious a one as with the rifle. If the handgun is going to be carried outside regularly as well, go with a regular premium hollowpoint round, since you can't know when the bad guys are coming to change things out.

Where shotguns are concerned, 12 or 20 gauge is most recommended. If you can, run the twelve. It offers a wider variety of ammunition than is available for the 20 gauge shotgun. Of that variety of ammunition, buckshot not less than #1 in size is the recommended load if you're going to load buckshot. (You have already read my opinion about loading birdshot or rubber rounds or similar loads earlier in this book. Let me repeat that opinion succinctly here: I wouldn't, and I wouldn't recommend that anyone else do that.) Otherwise, there are slugs of various types or even commercial variants of the 'buck and ball' load that's been around for who-knows-how long. All of these are worth thinking about for the home-defense shotgun.

Ignore manufacturer claims about their specialty ammunition not penetrating barriers. Always assume that it will go through more than anyone claims it will. Plan your patterns and lines of fire accordingly.

Finally: <u>Assume that any round, no matter what the type, will go through more walls than anybody says it will. Plan your lines of fire as best you can with that in mind</u>. You can also position furniture or other items with an eye to slowing down or stopping rounds if you're of a mind to consider that.

Tactics and Techniques: Some additional perspective.

I will not review the standard techniques of house-clearing. That information is readily available. If you have not already, seek out that information and learn it well; it is the basis on which I will build on in the rest of this essay. What I will do is offer some ideas to add to that basis for you to consider and experiment with, and, if they work for you, make your own.

I will remind you first: If you don't HAVE to move, it's usually best not to. Bunker up, cover the entrance, wait for help. But if you're forced to move for any reason, consider these ideas:

The 'Third-Eye' Principle: Moving fast, moving slow, sprinting, creeping, carefully pieing corners and doorways, doing a peek-and-run, pistol or long-gun, in all things at all times LEAD WITH THE WEAPON. The muzzle of the gun becomes like a third eye; where you look, there the sights go, there the muzzle points. Make it unthinking and automatic. You **must** keep focus and be able to exercise strict trigger/firing discipline if you are going to use this technique. Don't try it outside a training area unless you can.

Third Eye with rifle. Muzzle follows your eye wherever you look.

Third Eye with pistol (using a close-hold as would be likely when operating indoors). What you see, you should be able to shoot. Focus and concentration is essential to maintain fire discipline when using this technique.

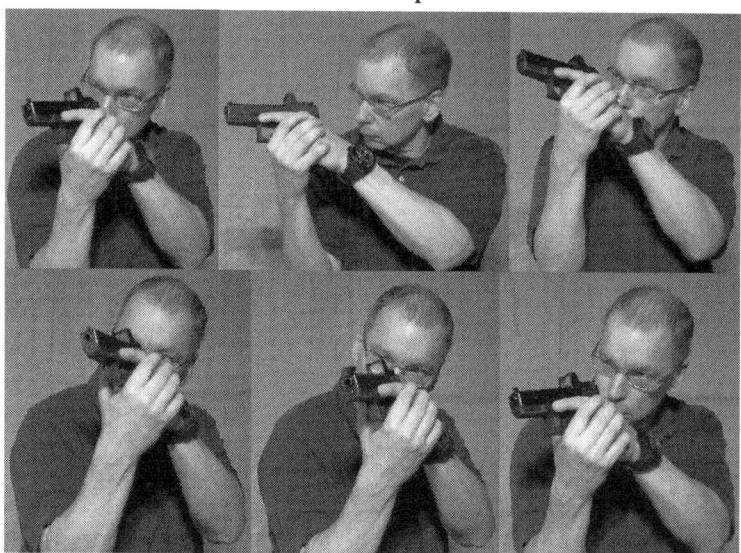

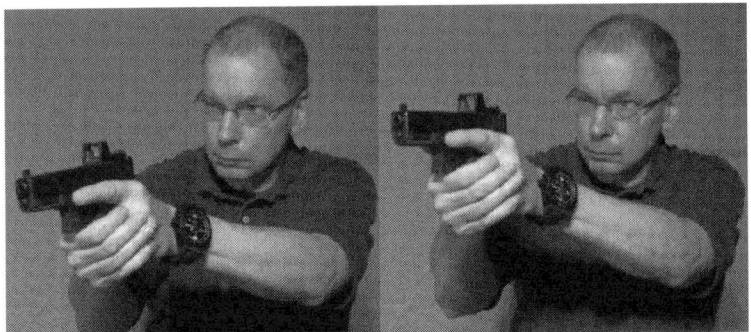

The Third Eye principle can also be used with Contact Ready positions as demonstrated with pistol (above) and rifle (below). Keeping a shallow angle and vertical sight alignment with the shooting eye allows you to fire an immediate shot at need that at close range will impact between the lower chest and hip-pelvis area. (Try this to know where you're hitting and from how far away you can hit before you employ this technique.) This can give you time and space to bring the gun up for a follow-up aimed shot if necessary.

The same principle is applicable to Close-Contact Ready position as demonstrated here. Keep the gun level and in the vertical sight-line. If needed, a shot can be triggered here or the gun can be quickly driven out under control to full extension.

Folding the stock as shown here is a trade-off. You gain a reduction in length and more maneuverability, but you lose the four points of contact and still have to use both hands to run the gun. You likely will not be able to maneuver the gun as quickly and surely as you could a pistol and it will more rapidly tire you out, not something you want to have happen too quickly in a fight for life.

Weapon control and muzzle discipline especially when using the Third Eye principle is very important and a key reason why I recommend that you don't fold the stock on a long gun even if you can. It still requires two hands to maneuver and without the extra points of support, it gets heavy fast and is harder to defend against a grab besides being harder to manage during movement such as searches. I like collapsible stocks for indoor use. You can shorten them for easier maneuvering and retain the multi-point support. A short spell of discomfort from the shorter-stock position some will feel is still better than the effort required to keep a long-gun with stock folded in play throughout a fight of unknown duration.

Be able to shoot with either hand/from either side: It reduces exposure when approaching doors and corners, makes it easier to use cover and concealment, is vital if the normal shooting hand is hurt, and offers you additional tactical options. Work to become comfortable and competent with either hand, and be able to switch sides at will with any weapon.

Being able to switch sides with confidence and efficiency is not just something to learn for emergencies. Being able to switch hands provides you tactical choices that you would not otherwise have available.

Be able to go slow or to GO-GO-GO!! You may not have the luxury of taking 15 minutes to slice the pie on a doorway or carve a corner with millimetric precision. You may have to rely on the reaction lag-time of the bad guy behind the wall. You may have to depend on the fact that you're initiating action and they're reacting to it. Understand that going faster is going to dramatically increase the danger you face going through a building with hostiles in it. But if the alternative is go fast or get dead, there are some things that might help you to live through it.

Learn to 'sneak a peek' quickly, practice getting a look with the smallest possible exposure in the smallest possible time, make use of the Third Eye, lead with the weapon, practice moving in lunges and bursts, covering a few feet at a time quickly, learn to move as quietly as possible even at speed (noise can be reduced more than you think) and consider the next idea that I don't see covered much when this subject is discussed...

Learn to use the vertical axis: Whenever I see someone demonstrating cornering or clearing in general, I see their muzzle go up and down and their line of vision go up and down. What I don't see is <u>them</u> going up and down. Why not? Think of what the bad guy crouched in the corner looking at the doorway is likely to expect and be waiting for—someone coming through, maybe in a combat crouch, but <u>upright</u>. Eyes and weapon will both be looking for that, waiting for the movement that will trigger their shot.

Examples of ways to run the vertical. In this case, two ways of rolling out low to either take a look (and any opportunity shot I may get) or to make the shot already decided on. Flexibility and core strength will be definite assets in situations like this.

This gives you some possibilities. Enter or cross the doorway as low as you can in a lunge or fast duck-walk movement as you engage. Roll out from the corner or into the doorway, acquire and shoot, roll back—sit back, shoot, sit up, in other words. Show them what they're looking for and do something else. For example, squat or kneel low, hold a flashlight as high up as you can to do the threat/ID scan. Cross the edge, flash the light, cross back low now that you know where they are to engage. There are surely other possibilities I haven't thought of.

Some of you won't be able to work the vertical line for various reasons. For those that can, or those that can get to where they can, look at it. It will give you some options you didn't have before.

Take the targets of opportunity. Don't wait for an ideal shot: If the first thing you see when clearing a corner is the bad guy's gun, put your sights on it and shoot. Damage to the gun or gun hand could get you as clear as a hit to his CNS and may not expose you to his shot as much to take it. Or if you see a shoulder or part of the body, why not go ahead and put a hole in it <u>if you are sure it is a bad guy</u>. Understand that <u>if you do not have positive target identification you do not shoot</u>. Period. Given positive target ID, almost any hit on him has a chance of reducing his ability to kill you and increasing your odds of getting out alive. But you need to be able to make that precision shot to do it.

Most any damage you can deliver will help you and hurt them. Even if you can't get the shot you want, be ready to take whatever shot you can get. You have to have the precision-shot-skills down to do it, though. Do you?

Make sure you can before you have to.

So there's the partial synopsis and the way I see it. Home Defense made easy? I <u>know</u> you don't believe <u>that</u>. And I know you don't believe that this is all there is to it. But maybe this helps to make it more likely you'll survive the experience. I hope it does, anyway.

More than that, I hope you never have to find out whether it's helpful or not.

RIGHT HAND, LEFT HAND, ONE HAND, BOTH HANDS, EITHER HAND

Ambidextrous training is like some medicine—it may be distasteful to you, but it helps you to take it anyway.

I have not always been as much an advocate of ambidextrous training with firearms—doing the same exercises and drills with both hands from both sides with rifle and pistol—as I have been over the past three or four years. On the other hand, I have done more gun*fight*-focused and tactical training in the last four years than I have in the ten or twenty preceding that and—to paraphrase Mark Twain—training as if you are going to be in a fight at any time you step out of your house, and sometimes if you don't, has a wonderful way of focusing the mind. And one of the things that it focused my mind on was that it is helpful—not absolutely necessary, perhaps, but very helpful—to be able to swap hands at will with confidence that I can be at least adequate for the fight with that other hand.

A couple of years ago at the time of this writing, a polite question was raised about my advocacy of ambidextrous training on a closed forum where I was a member (it was shut down). I repeat the bulk of the well-done argument here:

"Although we typically use the term "strong side," what we're really talking about is dominant side. Except for a very small percentage of the population who are truly ambidextrous, human brains are wired to favor one side or the other. When the brain gets inconsistent images from both eyes, it picks one and deletes the inconsistent portion; the one it chooses is the dominant eye. When we learn to write, most of us chose one hand or the other. Some may have been forced or biased toward the right hand by parents or teachers, but about 90% choose that side naturally. Regardless of how much you train or practice, you will always be better with one side than the other."

The person who posted that is almost certainly right.

I DON'T CARE.

DO IT ANYWAY.

Another poster, also an instructor, put it this way on that same thread:

"It's in the wiring..."

She's almost certainly right too.

I DON'T CARE.

DO IT ANYWAY.

Many times when the subject is raised, on that forum and every other one I've been on where it was discussed, one or more people will write that they won't ever be as good with one hand/one side as with the other.

That may be true and it likely is with most people.

I DON'T CARE.

DO IT ANYWAY.

Train to go left, train to go right, at will or on demand, with rifle and pistol. It will be good for you.

Here's why:

It adds an element of variety to your training. Even though you may be doing the same thing on one side as on the other, because of the difference in mental and physical dexterity that most of us have between sides, it can often be like learning something new. Switching sides and becoming as dexterous as you can pushes you out of your comfort zone and out of the box of complacency you risk falling into by doing the same things over and over. Looked at the right way, this can be a whole new experience for you to explore and enjoy.

It's a way to challenge yourself. You're looking at the same thing, but somehow it's different; you're doing the same thing, but somehow it's different. There's some stress generated and some effort, like when you were just learning something for the first time. There's some uncertainty, too: Can you do it? Can you move the skills over? How good can you get? Think of it—without spending any money, without adding significant time, you're having to focus again and work out the movement again. You both learn and reinforce what you know at the same time. It can be hard, but isn't that the way some training should be? We can't prepare for hard things by doing easy things; we have to prepare for hard things by doing things as hard or harder. Changing sides is an easy way to make things hard again. And when you do…

Doing it, training each side as far up as you can, gives you confidence and reduces fear. Consider that some training is not designed so much to instill a skill into the trainee as it is to condition the trainee to continue to act and move and try and do under conditions of stress, uncertainty, and fear. That conditioning is not as specific as skill training, and so the mind, under real-world conditions of stress, uncertainty, and fear is less likely to freeze up or get so confused and distracted that the person can't act. It's not the same degree of stress, but making yourself work through the awkwardness and frustration and even initial failure you may face shifting hands helps overall with other things. When you are faced with some other confusing or awkward or stressful situation, the subconscious calls on all those things you have been through, including this, and says to itself, "I have done that; I can do this. I have faced things like this before; I can do it again." And so you don't freeze from uncertainty. You act. Doing hard things makes it easier to do other hard things.

Having even a limited capability to switch hands gives you options you did not have before. If you don't practice it, you don't know if you can even do it, and you don't know how well, how much, or when it is best to do it. If you haven't done it even to a degree, you probably won't think about doing it when it brings you an advantage or reduces disadvantage. Physical ability, then, gives you mental flexibility and choices that could make the difference in whether you live or die. In the fight, options and flexibility are good.

It gives you a way to surprise or confuse the attacker. We live in a right-handed world and we expect things to go in a right-handed way. That's the reality of it. The attacker is most likely going to be right-handed, and the attacker is most likely going to expect the would-be victim to be the same way. The ability to either start with the left hand or to switch quickly and with confidence to left-handed employment could be just enough edge to get the initiative back and win the fight. Left-handers are troublesome to right-handers in a number of sports. Offering the same kind of switch-hitting trouble to your attacker could work to your advantage. (Natural lefties, realize that you have this edge and bask in the glory of it as much as you wish, but keep training regardless. It's a potential edge, not a guaranteed fight-winner.) It may not be a big advantage, but it may be enough to make a difference.

You need to be ready to do it if you're forced to. This is usually the first reason offered for working with the other hand—that you might take a hit in the dominant side and have to switch over. Most people nod their heads in agreement, run a few minutes of other-side drills occasionally and call it Good. *Is it? Is it good enough to get you through a hit to the 'good' side? Is it good enough to carry you through days or weeks in a sling following an injury and immobilization?* (I've carried when one arm was in a cast. At the time I was doing that, if I had had to run the gun in a fight, I likely would have not been able to do it well enough to survive.) Is it enough, in other words, to *live* with?

"You're talking worst-case situation," you might say, "it doesn't happen that often." Neither does a gunfight or an attack where we would have to use a gun to defend ourselves, but we train for that. We, gun-carriers, are an optimistic kind of pessimist. We have a positive attitude because we prepare, mentally and physically, to survive the worst-case situations. And there *are* cases where defenders have taken hits in the gun-hand and had to switch to survive. If training for it provides the other benefits listed besides this very important one, why not add mirror-image practice to your schedule?

So you see the *why* of it…what about the *how* of it? How can you better prepare for the necessity, or choice, of switching to the other side to run the gun with? The most obvious way is to run parallel sets of drills and practice routines. You don't have to immediately double the number of repetitions of an exercise or double the training time, either. Begin with a one in five or one in four ratio in time spent or in repetitions run. Gradually increase that until its 1:1 and continue from there. Another option is to schedule 'broken wing' sessions where you force yourself to do everything start to finish with or from the other side.

Something else you can do is to switch sides sometimes in day-to-day activity. We all favor one hand or another for lots activities like eating or brushing our teeth or combing our hair. Occasional movement to the other side, or something like a half-page of 'abcs' done with the non-writing hand now and again, can help to move us to general dexterity in mind and body that will help us to get *ambi*dexterity with the gun.

Hard? Maybe so, for some. But it's *important*. That's why we do things like this even when they *are* hard.

Because there may come a day…

NICE DRAWSTROKE: CAN YOU DO THAT ONE-HANDED?

You may have been knocked down or almost knocked down and caught yourself. You may be holding on to something to keep yourself from falling. You may be pulling someone behind you or pulling yourself in front of someone, or pushing someone out of the way. You may have hurt your other arm, the one that normally clears the cover. You may be blocking or fending off an attack.

And you may have to draw your weapon while you're doing any of these things.

The Really Important Question is: Can you? The Life Saving Answer needs to be: YES.

Here are some things to help you do that.

Talking to a friend, see a threat, you have to move him and help yourself past him and engage. A good reason to have the 'one-hander' ready to go.

SAFETY FIRST. EMPTY GUN, FAKE GUN, AIRSOFT GUN WHEN YOU BEGIN PRACTICING THIS. It's hard to be too heavy on this emphasis. As you will see, there is an increased likelihood that you'll have to deal with clothing snags. Part of the learning process involves learning to work around and through them. DO IT EMPTY AND SLOW FIRST, JUST LIKE WHEN YOU WERE LEARNING THE DRAWSTROKE IN THE BEGINNING. When you're ready to speed up, use Airsoft if you have it. If not, keep the empty gun empty for a while. Slow back down, SLOW BACK DOWN WHEN YOU START DOING THIS LIVE-FIRE.

Don't skip steps, don't rush the process. Guard your life in training the same way you guard your life on the street, with full alertness and awareness of what's going on.

To work through clothing snags on the gun, think muzzle down, punch down, and small circles of the muzzle and hand to get the muzzle first and then the rest of the gun out of the clothing. The pictures in this section will provide some guidance about that.

That said, let's look at the drawstroke....

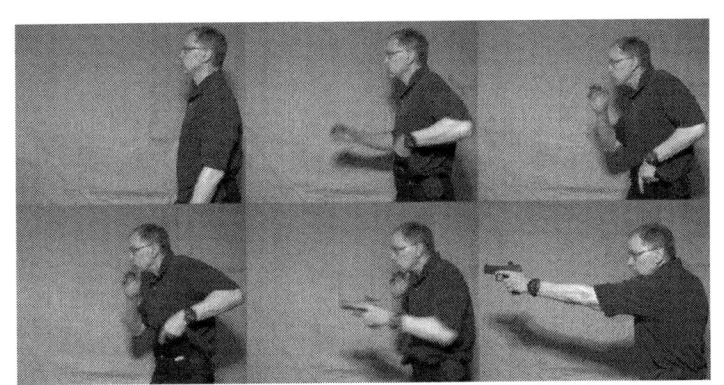

Here's the basic idea: Get the gun out and start shooting, but do it with one hand. That means you have to clear the cover, then get the grip and draw the gun before the cover falls back to get in the way of the draw.

There are a couple of things you have to be aware of that may happen that will force adjustments to the presentation and the shot(s) or that will necessitate the equivalent of a failure drill for the drawstroke. Both problems derive from not beating the cover back down to the gun or not keeping it clear as you drive your hand down to get the grip. Top picture shows one possibility, which is your thumb may hook into the tail of the shirt as you draw.

The quickest solution is to extend the gun as far as you can while keeping it in the vertical sight-line and shoot. This is where point-shooting training and practice will come into its own in a life-saving way. Going ahead with the shot is advised because the nature of this kind of snag makes clearing the shirt off the thumb take too much time. (Your attacker is not going to wait for you to get clear. Remember that. You're not knights on a field of chivalrous battle. Don't expect fair play, and don't provide it to someone that's trying to kill you.) Where the shirt is snagged at, it is unlikely to interfere with either the grip or with shooting.

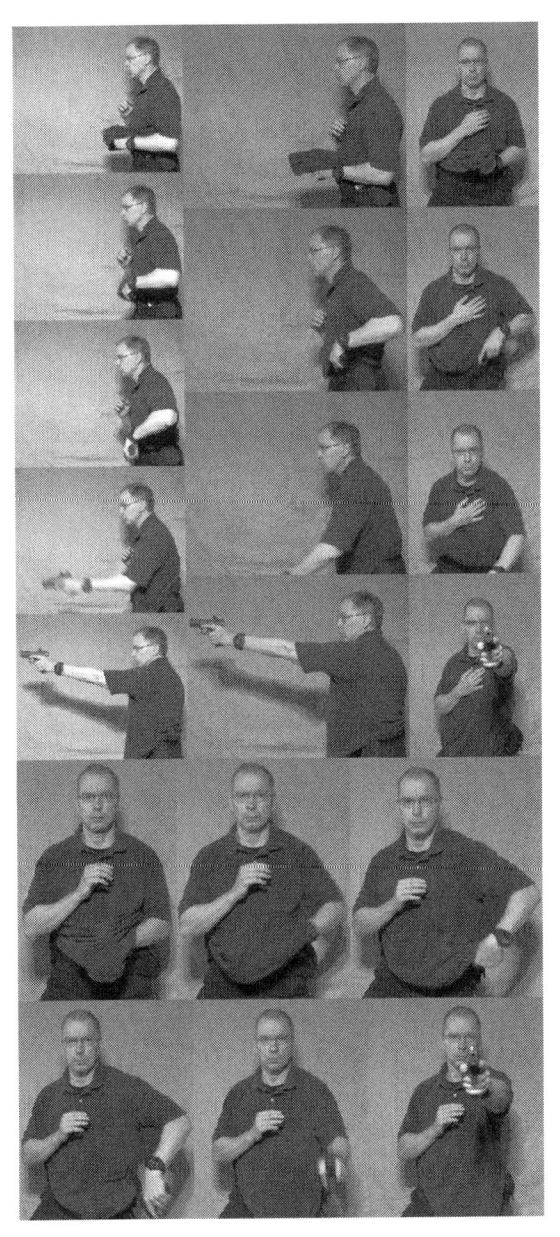

Something that sometimes happens even when you have a hand just to clear the shirt with is that the gun gets caught underneath the shirt. You will probably feel what's going on as soon as it happens.

There are three ways to deal with this when it occurs. One way to deal with the snag is to immediately point the gun straight down and drive it toward the ground and out from under the shirt. It doesn't have to clear all the way down before you can raise it to firing position and take the shot. Another solution is to immediately circle the muzzle, rotating around the wrist, turning the gun in and then circling it out and away from the shirt and into extension as shown here.

There are a couple of things you have to be aware of that may happen that will force adjustments to the presentation and the shot(s) or that will necessitate the equivalent of a failure drill for the drawstroke. Both problems derive from not beating the cover back down to the gun or not keeping it clear as you drive your hand down to get the grip. Top picture shows one possibility, which is your thumb may hook into the tail of the shirt as you draw.

The quickest solution is to extend the gun as far as you can while keeping it in the vertical sight-line and shoot. This is where point-shooting training and practice will come into its own in a life-saving way. Going ahead with the shot is advised because the nature of this kind of snag makes clearing the shirt off the thumb take too much time. (Your attacker is not going to wait for you to get clear. Remember that. You're not knights on a field of chivalrous battle. Don't expect fair play, and don't provide it to someone that's trying to kill you.) Where the shirt is snagged at, it is unlikely to interfere with either the grip or with shooting.

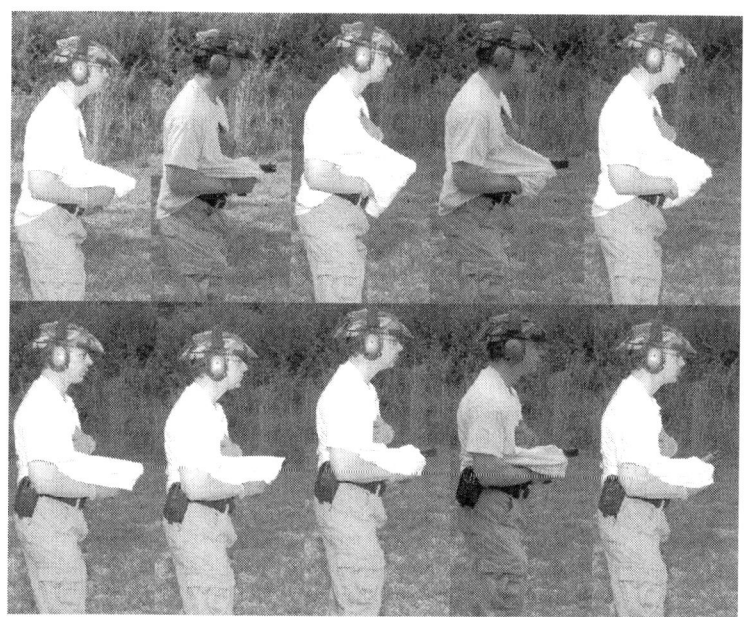

Another way to deal with the snag is to extend the gun under and inside the shirt as far as you can while keeping the vertical sight-line and start pulling the trigger. Again, point-shooting skills come into their own in this situation. (The sequence shown here is a combination of three runs done for the photos for this book.) There is an increased risk of malfunction, of course, but repeated trials have demonstrated that the gun will not necessarily jam after one shot. In fact, in all the times I have done this with either a stock pistol or the RMR-equipped Glock used in this sequence, I have never fired less than three times, and could have emptied the magazine at will in most cases.

THE FLOATING GUN
If you're going to take your point shooting skills as far as the fight needs them to be, you've got to have it.

I see them over and over again, and I still do it myself sometimes (not nearly as often as I used, but I still catch myself on rare occasion). I see them at classes, on the range practicing, in groups, watching others work, and when working by myself. Once you know what to look for they're pretty easy to spot. They're like chronic or recurring illnesses.

I call them the Welded Hand Syndrome and Locked-In-Position Syndrome.

Welded-Hand Syndrome is characterized by a strong and determined unconscious reluctance to release the support hand from the grip of the gun. The shooter beset by Welded-Hand Syndrome acts as if his or her hands have been super-glued and duct-taped to the grip such that they are unable to let go and shoot with one hand despite the position they are in or the angle to the target they are engaging. They will twist and turn and step, bend and flex, and move the wrong way trying to keep their gun on the target, unaware that they are in the grip of the Welded-Hand Syndrome.

Related to and often seen in conjunction with Welded-Hand Syndrome is Locked-In-Position Syndrome. LIPS is characterized by the unthinking drive to keep a pre-set arm and upper-body shooting position under any and all circumstances and no matter where the target is or how they are moving (if they're moving) whether it is appropriate to the circumstances or not.

WHS and LIPS do occur in isolation but will most often be observed coming up together. Both syndromes have the same three primary causes: A lack of experience or training, a history of training that is totally or almost totally devoted to the proactive gunfight, and the natural tendency we all have to want to remain squared up to something or someone that is trying to kill us.

Diagnosis of either or both conditions involves observation of the shooter in question to answer these questions: Is the position and placement of the gun appropriate to what the shooter needs to be doing with it? Does the shooter appear to be 'bound up' or in an awkward position? Is the shooter moving more slowly and awkwardly than they should be or in a different direction than they intend or that is appropriate to the situation? If the answers are 'No', 'Yes' and 'Yes', then WHS or LIPS should be suspected. Further observation is then necessary to confirm the presence and severity of the conditions.

Effects of these conditions range from being personally frustrated about your ability to easily get good hits on a target that's other than directly in front of you to your being killed in a fight because you can't maneuver properly, move too slowly, are unable to get the gun into line like you need to, or from ineffective use of cover that exposes too much of your body to incoming fire. Given the potential severity of the effects, serious thought should be given as to how to avoid falling victim to these conditions. Fortunately, effective treatments are available and are simple, though not always easy for some, to apply.

Top picture in sequence is the core of the problem with LIPS and WHS: An overwhelming urge to keep this grip on the pistol no matter what you're doing. Example shown here is of a left-handed shooter severely afflicted with LIPS and WHS doing a walking drill to right and left. Going right, they have to crank the pistol over awkwardly to maintain the grip and some semblance of the arm position. Going left, they end up crabbing sideways to maintain grip and position.

This sideways movement may be a viable option if you are wearing body armor. Otherwise, it slows down and disrupts evasive movement, opens a larger target area to return fire, and could turn you away from the cover you were running for.

Treatments are both corrective and preventive and may need to be applied on an ongoing basis. Treatments are as follows:

Learning and practicing ambidextrous use of all weapons. (At the least, getting as near to full ambidexterity as is possible.)

Learning and practicing one-handed shooting (of the handgun).

Learning and practicing to be able to shoot accurately with the gun below the eye-line, in other than dead-ahead directions, and held at distances ranging from in contact with your body to full extension.

The aim of the treatments is to develop the Floating Gun. This is a state in which you will automatically and without much if any conscious thought put the gun at the level you need and extended to the distance required in any direction of the clock face as the situation and the target you are engaging dictate. Sometimes one-handed, sometimes not, sometimes in one hand, sometimes in the other, sometimes held far away and sometimes in contact with your body, high, low, in-between, getting hits where you need them as you move where you need to without binding, bending, or twisting unnaturally. Furthermore, that point, that extension, that position, that direction, can and will change the moment the situation changes and the moment your relationship to the target changes. As you turn, as you change direction, as you change levels or speed or distance, or as the target does, so does your gun. It goes where it needs to be so that it can do what you need it to do.

Examples of recommended solutions to LIPS and WHS: Train yourself to automatically and naturally release the support and to go one-handed, to switch hands as required or desirable, and to shoot from compressed positions and different angles and orientations of the weapon. Example here shows a right-handed shooter moving left and right.

You need to learn to float the rifle as well. Example here is the end of a simple standing drill that starts with the rifle in a low underarm assault position. As the shooter moves from underarm assault to standard shooting position where sights are acquired, a string of shots is directed up the centerline of the target.

To best develop and keep updated on the use of the Floating Gun concept, therapy under the guidance of a qualified instructor is highly recommended. Ongoing practice and training and refresher training is advisable, as without re-emphasis of the concept, Welded-Hand and Locked-In Syndrome will often re-occur. It's happened to me; don't let it happen to you.

I'll get a bit more serious now: I believe there are two fundamentals that should not change no matter what you're doing with the gun, and one fundamental that almost never should but can sometimes. The two things that should not change are your grip (the way you grip, not the tension of the grip), whether one or two-handed, and the way you work the trigger. These two things should always be consistent. The one fundamental that should almost not change is eye-hand, or eye-weapon, alignment. Even if the gun is below your line of sight, it should as much as possible be aligned with the visual centerline or master eye in order to have the best chance of hitting the intended target. As long as these fundamentals are satisfied, then the gun should be allowed to 'float' to where it will best get the hits you need.

Being able to float the gun does more for you than just to enable you to make hits from any position in any direction in an emergency, though that would be more than enough to justify the acquisition of the capability. Where employed deliberately, ambidextrous and one-handed facility with the weapon specifically will give you tactical options you will not have otherwise. For all these reasons, having the ability to float the gun is an all but must-have skill to everyone that carries and a definite must-have skill for the serious student of the gunfight.

Take the time, make the effort, get the skill, and learn the Floating Gun. You will not regret it.

CONSISTENCY, THE CONCEPT

A friend of mine who has gone to a several different schools and many classes once told me that he had been taught more than six different ways to do a chamber check.

I remember being very mildly shocked. I mean, seriously—<u>six</u> ways? <u>More</u> than six ways? To check the chamber of a pistol?

Would any of you like to bet that my friend uses more than one, maybe two, of all the ways he knows to make that chamber check?

As an instructor, I feel an obligation to be familiar with different ways of doing the same thing so that I can understand whatever a student may bring to a class. As an instructor, I also feel an obligation to provide that student a proven and consistent method of doing any given thing to simplify their learning and retention process.

As a student and as someone who wants to go home after the fight is over, I believe that finding one or the smallest number of proven methods, and then making them consistent and automatic, is key to my ability to survive.

Consistency as a concept encompasses two areas in my view. One is to settle on techniques that work for you best and are as simple as they can be and still get the job done. (Roger Phillips: It's not 'Keep It Simple, Stupid', it's "Keep It As Simple As It Needs To Be") My friend may know more than one way to do a chamber check, but I bet he practices only one way to actually do that, and I bet he doesn't think about how to do it now; he just checks the chamber and goes on about his business with the gun.

Choice of technique and procedure is the element of consistency that most people think of first and sometimes the only element of consistency they think of, period. The other element of consistency I want you to consider is consistency across platforms, techniques, and methods.

Back to the chamber check idea: Do you use an over-the-slide grip or a slingshot grip to check the chamber? Now, what grip do you use to rack the slide? If they are different, you're not being consistent in concept. It's not the same exact grip you use for both, no, but the idea is that you're using an overhand, or slingshot, (or reverse-hand-friction-hold or Indonesian gun-ninja technique if you want), with small variations, whenever you are running the slide. Practicing one is, to some extent, practicing both. This means you can make practice time more beneficial and efficient and cut down on the amount of conscious thought necessary to run the gun when you're pressed for time and space.

Grip is another example. Lots of us have and work with both revolvers and semi-autos. Two-handed grip can't be the same on both, but by varying the position of the thumbs a little it will be close to the same and so will be easier to transition between them. If you go with the thumb-behind-thumb grip on the revolver, though, there is a risk of doing that without thinking when you have a semi-auto in hand, with painful results; likewise, if you go thumbs straight out on both semi-auto and revolver. With minor variations, though, you have enough cross-platform grip consistency that the transition is fast and unthinking, and you won't get hurt besides. What's not to like about that?

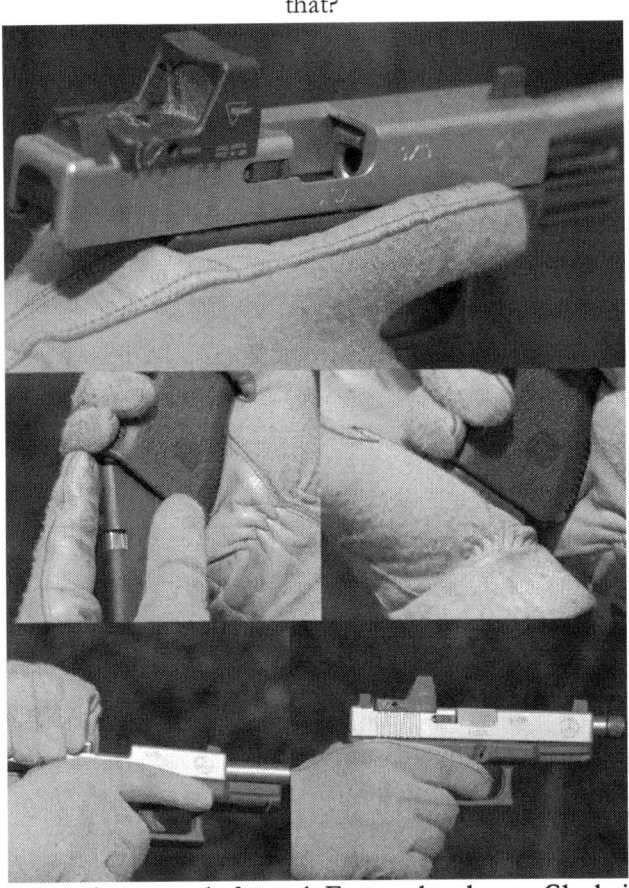

Consistency between platforms 1: Empty chamber on Glock, insert magazine, seat firmly, run the slide, ready to fire.

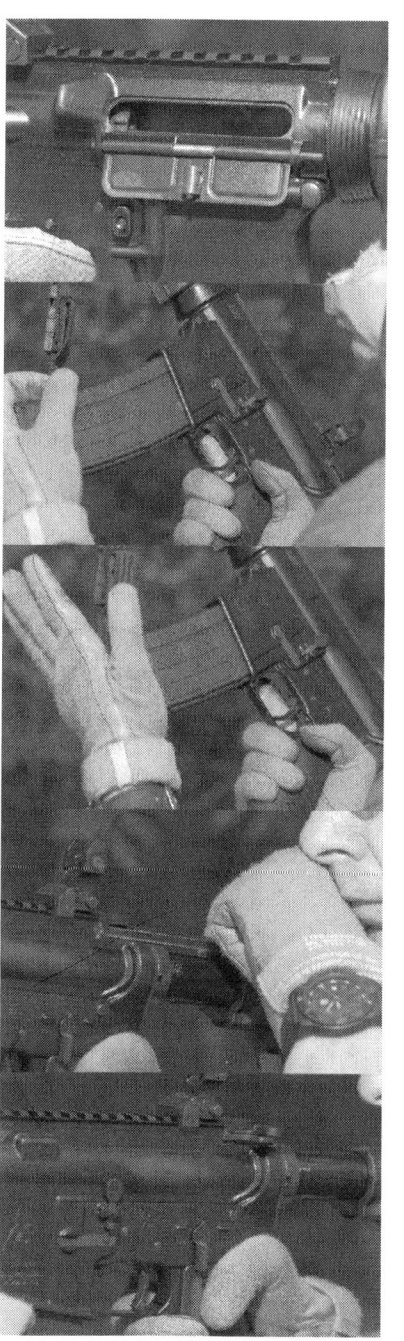

Final example: Basic malfunction drill. A Glock goes click, I do a slam-rack; smack the base of the mag, rack the slide. One, two, it works or not, I go to something else if not. A simple thing, drilled so that it's consistent, and it works with every semi-auto I've ever had in my hand.

Consistency between platforms 2: Empty chamber on AR, insert magazine, seat firmly, run the bolt, ready to fire. Differences in detail, yes, but primary movements and the base concept is the same between them.

Now I pick up an AR, I'm shooting, it goes click. I can do S.P.O.R.T.S., or I can slam-rack as a first reaction. What do you think I'll do without thinking? Exactly. Smack the base of the mag, run the bolt, see if it shoots. Same as I do with the Glock. It's what I did with an AR, in fact, when I had not fired one for over a year and had a malfunction. I did it because it's what I do with weapons that load that way (magazine straight in).   Consistency across platforms. Consistency of technique and method.

Now, you can't apply this concept rigidly. I won't slam-rack an AK when it stops shooting, for example. You can't apply the concept across every platform or with every technique and method. You might even deliberately avoid consistency in some cases. For example: You might use a completely different grip with that chamber-check so that you are reminded that you are doing a chamber-check and not some other, totally different, manipulation of the gun. It can be carried too far. Remember what Roger says: As simple as it needs to be. No simpler than that.

With some thought, however, the concept of consistency of technique, of method, and across platforms will enhance your training, save time, increase your skill and competency faster, and maybe get you done with the fight and home to your family when you're falling back on what you've trained to do and what's in your motor memory.

So, sure--if you're interested and you enjoy doing it, maybe learn some extra ways of doing things. But keep an eye on, and practice, the smaller number of things that 1) work best for you and 2) work across as many areas and platforms as possible. Certainly look at new ideas you are presented with, and if they're really better for you, don't hesitate to bring them in to your toolbox. Do be sure to spend extra time and extra repetition on the new idea before you can be sure of making it consistent.

Narrow the focus, enlarge the capability. Practice consistency.

Now go get some training.

THERE'S ONLY ONE WAY...

Keeping a semi-auto fed. It's been on my mind lately. I've been going over the three reloading techniques, one of which has two variations.

Something started to nag me, though. It took me a while to work out what. Here's the question that told me what was nagging me:

What is the similarity between each apparently-separate technique of changing magazines in a semi-auto pistol?

I don't remember the answer taking a long time to form, but it did take some time: The same thing happens at the pistol. That is, *you do the same thing with the magazine you're loading and with the pistol no matter what technique you're using to reload.* You index the magazine you're loading, finger over the top round; hand finds hand; line the magazine up and SLAM it into positive lock; RACK the slide; get back into the fight.

THIS is the important part. THIS is what has to be handled correctly, concisely, consistently. <u>Every time.</u>

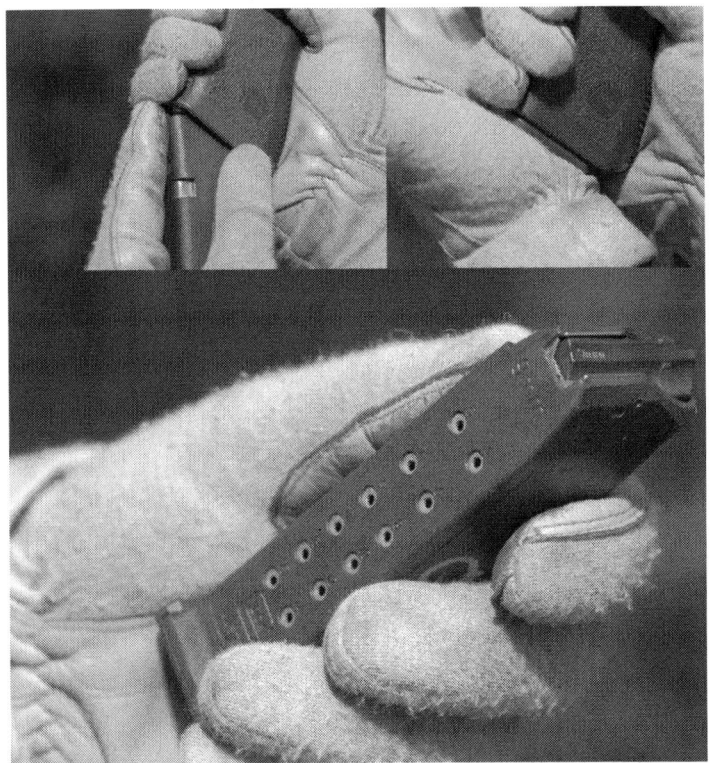

What you do with the empty magazine is not nearly as important as what you do with the full one when your gun is empty and the fight is still on.

It doesn't change, no matter what technique or method you're using.

If that doesn't change; if what you do to actually load the pistol is the same thing, then is it really three different methods (plus one variation), or one method with four variations?

What makes the variation? What you do with the magazine, whether empty or partially loaded, that comes out of the pistol.

If you drop it, it's a speed reload; if you catch the empty magazine and put it away somewhere, it's a reload with retention; if you pull the partially-empty mag, tuck it away, and load a full mag, it's one variation of the tactical reload; if you get the fully-loaded mag before you pull the partial mag out of the gun, it's another variation of the tactical reloadNot too hard, when you think about it that way.

I realize that some will say that since you don't normally run the slide when doing a tactical reload, it should be considered a separate technique. It's a legitimate point. I do note that I often run the slide even in tactical reloads because it's practiced more. I would bet that other people have the same kind of default. If that's true, then we have just the one technique with four variations.

This simplifies things for me considerably. I only have to really worry about getting that one IMPORTANT technique done under the stress of someone trying to kill me. As long as I do the main technique, what happens with the variations is not so important.
Maybe. Hard to tell when a small thing will become a large thing when the fight is on, I would say.

In the meantime, I offer here this simplification for you to consider and make use of if you want to.

PORTING A CARRY GUN IS A BAD IDEA

Porting is the practice of cutting slots at the end of the barrel so that gas is directed up and, usually, to either side of the barrel at slight angles when the gun is fired. This is done to reduce recoil and allow for better control and recovery time between shots. This sounds like a good idea if you're shooting in defense of life--shoot faster and be surer of getting back on target. But it's not something you should do. Here's why:

Take your carry weapon and put it in three positions. One, on the hip as if you had leveled it right out of the holster to make a fast close-range shot. Second position is to bring it up to what is usually called the Number-2 position of the four-count draw-stroke or the pectoral index--thumb against the side of the chest, gun angled slightly out. Again, this is a position you might take for a close-range shot against an attacker in arm's reach or coming in on you. Third position is what is sometimes called close-contact or the Number-3 position of the four-count: two hand hold but gun drawn in as close to the sternum as your arms and wrists will allow.

In each position, look down and note where the end of the slide or barrel is at the muzzle end. That's where the ports will be cut, and that's where the hot gases and hot unburned powder will come from out of that port, some of which are likely to go into your face and eyes when you fire from that position.

The technical term for the results of that in a fight for life is Not Good.

Also, in low-light or full-dark conditions, the flash from the ports is large and bright and won't help your ability to see things after the first shot or two. But the flash is going to be there even without porting; there may just be more of it. The main problem is the stuff in your face from a close-in shot.

So: Port competition-only weapons if you want. Port hunting weapons if you want. Port weapons you won't ever carry for self-defense if you want. You can control where and how you shoot those. But for the defensive weapon, where you won't have control of the circumstances where you will have to shoot it to save your life?

Don't do it.

SELF-DEFENSE WITH THE LONG GUN:*
Considering the concept.

As long as I'm talking about my friend up north...

I mentioned that he likes rifles. Has three, and a shotgun, as far as I know. Maybe more, but at least that many. Likes shooting them. Really likes the concept of being a rifleman--that focused, precise, accurate long-gunner that's part of American history and maybe of American mythology.

One of the problems he's having, though, is that he's talking to me about it. Remember me? Mr. "It's The Fight, Silly!" me?

Once again, I'm thinking he probably practices more with his rifle than I do currently, and that he can most likely shoot it better than I can.

What he hasn't done to date, as far as I know, is to take a rifle off of the 100 (or better) yard range and into a pistol pit and run the same drills with his rifle as he does with his pistol. I've done that. And I'm recommending to him, and to you, that you do the same thing with whatever long-gun you have chosen to keep ready as a home-defense weapon.

You may wonder why I recommend that. Here is my thinking:

Whenever the subject of defending yourself and family with a rifle comes up on the few gun forums I monitor, someone almost invariably reminds us that it is unlikely that we would be able to justify shooting someone that was fifty or a hundred yards or more away. The 'imminent or immediate' part of the threat to life would be pretty hard to come by in most cases, they will say.
And as irritating as it may be to some of us reading that, they are correct in saying that. Not completely and absolutely, mind you-- exceptions will always be present that can test the rule--but pretty close to it.

If that's true, though--that legally you won't often get a practical benefit out of the rifle's additional range capability--then a reasonable question is: Why even have a long-gun available as a defensive weapon?

Heavy-hitting power and precision are two reasons to have a rifle, and the training to use it, available for defensive use.

There are two additional advantages that rifles and shotguns have over pistols besides range--power and precision. Pistols of almost any caliber have always been considered underpowered weapons whose only claim to desirability has been their handiness (and in modern times, their concealability). We don't carry pistols because we expect trouble, we carry them in case we get into trouble we don't see in time to get out of. If you know trouble is coming, the saying goes, get a rifle and get friends with rifles. Rifles and shotguns hit harder than pistols, and when someone is already inside the front door, hitting hard is what you want. You need them to stop as hard and as quickly as you can make them, and so you grab the long-gun when you can.

The longer sight radius and additional points of contact--shoulder and cheek--also makes for better precision shooting than with a pistol. And even shotguns need precision. Inside of the average home or even to the edge of the average front yard, even buckshot will not spread enough that you can just face somewhere toward the bad guy and close your eyes and still hit. And besides that, even rifles and shotguns work better and faster stopping bad guys if you get Central Nervous System hits; you need precision for that. And besides **that**, you have as much concern with hitting what you're aiming at and **only** what you're aiming at with a long-gun as you do with a pistol. So take advantage of that extra precision you get and practice using it at the ranges and under the circumstances you're most like to face in a defensive situation.

What ranges? What circumstances?

Range is easiest. What is the longest line of sight you have in your house or apartment? And, how far is it to the edges of your lawn or yard? In my case, 36 feet and 67 feet, the last my stepped-off measure to the opposite edge of the street in front of my house. Not quite the rifle shot my friend up north envisions, but nothing that law enforcement and military doesn't face every day either, and they do just fine with long-guns in those situations. If you've chosen a shotgun and buckshot for home defense, set targets at those ranges and room and hallway distances and make sure you know where the round you're using 'patterns'--the roughly-circular area that the shot will spread (or not) into. (You need to know this and may be surprised at the <u>lack</u> of spread at those short ranges, so get the patterning done ASAP. Better to be surprised on the range than in the fight.)

One thing to keep in mind with certain rifles as the range gets in very close: Certain rifles, patterned after military/police weapons, have a front sight post that's up to two inches above the line of the barrel. If you're sighting as normal at very close distances, the shot will go low. You need to work a little at the range to understand where to 'hold' the sight-line so that you hit where you want to hit when you're shooting from across the room.

The circumstances where you might use a rifle in defense fall into three categories in my thinking: Proactive, Reactive, and a kind of in-between that I'll call 'Prepared Reactive'.

Proactive is least likely. That would be any situation where you have enough warning to have the rifle or shotgun prepared to fight with. This would also be where you're more likely to have the longer ranges to deal with. An example would be a serious 'bump in the night' or noise outside somewhere while you're still awake.

Reactive, for most people, is more likely than Proactive but not as likely as 'Prepared Reactive'. An example would be some crazy person driving up out of the blue and shooting up your house, or a home invasion that comes in the front when you're in a room in the back of the house. There is time only to access the weapon and *fight*.

Prepared Reactive seems to me to be the most likely current circumstance where a rifle would be brought into play for defense. The best example is the standard recommendation for the 'bump in the night'--assume a defensive position in the safe room, cover the entrance with your rifle or shotgun, call for help, and wait it out. You're reacting to a possible threat, but with a plan you've prepared in advance and not on the instant.

There are many variations of these circumstances, but I believe that most if not all situations of self-defense with a long-gun will fall into one of those three categories.

So how do you prepare to actually *fight* with a rifle or shotgun?

The basic answer is to take the long-gun to the same range as you take your pistol, if that's allowed, and do the same kind of drills with it that you do with your pistol. You will have to change a few things, and there are some differences between having the long-gun in your hands instead of the pistol. Take note of these points in your training:

Obviously, you're not going to be drawing a rifle from concealment. Substitute two things for that. One is to practice presenting and firing the rifle from different ready positions such as Patrol Ready, Contact Ready, Underarm, and other positions.

Examples of ready positions: SUL, left, and Cradle, right. Moving from positions like this to the shot with the long-gun is equivalent to the drawstroke with the pistol and should be practiced in the same way.

Moving from positions like this to the shot with the long-gun is equivalent to the drawstroke with the pistol and should be practiced in the same way.

Also, set the rifle up as it is in your house, move yourself the approximate distance you would be away from it that you would be in different parts of your house, mark out the same route around 'corners' and through 'doors' as best as you are able, then work on accessing the weapon from a standing (or sitting) start--run the route, pick up the weapon, load or chamber if you don't normally have it ready to fire, then move back to where the target is and engage. Make the route and the placement as close to the real home as possible. Also, practice a 'covert ready'--simulate you in, for example, your front doorway with the long-gun out of sight beside the door. 'Draw' the weapon on the signal, chamber or disengage safeties, shoulder, aim, fire. When you dry-fire at home--why not do it with the long-gun as well?--walk through the access as you would do it in an emergency.

There are different situations where you would be compelled to be moving through your home with the rifle or shotgun in hand--you can't always set up in a barricaded place. Example situations are retreating back to the safe room after you've collected a family member, retreating back into the house under fire (and firing back) to get behind cover or concealment, and moving through the house to check out the bump you're not absolutely sure about or to collect family members to take them back to the safe room. If you even think you might need to do this for real, start practicing it now. You need to work out ready positions while moving in tight quarters (My main hallway is 37", my interior doors are 29"--add my body thickness to even the shortest legal rifle and careful movement and searching and pieing corners and doorways gets interesting very quickly. Ask me how I know.), how to move both forwards and backwards, think and work out some retention and close-combat techniques and generally 'wargame' the process as comprehensively as you can.

Train and practice the same things with the rifle as with the pistol, including, as in the example here, dynamically transitioning through shooting positions while maintaining steady and accurate fire as you change and during the transitions.

   You need also to be able to shoot the long-gun from either side and have malfunction clearance procedures in hand. Reloading techniques should, naturally, also be practiced. Understand also that what is cover for a pistol round is likely to be concealment for a shotgun or rifle round and set your plans for use of that accordingly.

Dynamic and evasive movement and accurate shooting while moving at speed are highly desirable skills to acquire with both handgun and long-gun.

That's about as much as I can recommend without getting too specific. I believe that these basic skill-sets, practiced dynamically and with imagination, could be of great value to you if ever the chips are down on your table.

Two thoughts in closing:

You still need to practice **shooting**, and you still need to practice--with the rifle, at least--at long range, 100 yards and more. The foundational skills of shooting are important for all firearms.

If you can get training in defensive use of the rifle or shotgun, do so, BUT GET TRAINING WITH THE HANDGUN FIRST. If you are ever forced to use a firearm to defend your life, it will most likely be the pistol. LEARN TO FIGHT WITH THE PISTOL FIRST. After that, seek formal training with the rifle or shotgun.

The summary is this: **Think FIGHT, no matter what the weapon you have.**

It could be important that you do.

It could be life or death.

*The use of the rifle specifically in the counter-offensive fight will be covered in more detail in Volume 3 of this series to be by the end of the second quarter of 2014.

HERE BEGINNETH THE LESSON

What?!?!?!...You think this is all there is to it?!?!?!

Learning never stops. That said…

Thank you for reading this.
Thank you for considering these ideas.

Thank you for starting, or for continuing, to develop yourself and your skills.
Don't stop here.

Keep going.

(See you in class.)

RESOURCES
Some places that will help you travel the path.

This section is about where to get stuff. Stuff for your mind: Knowledge, skills, ways and means of thinking, help with mindset and attitude. Stuff for your hand: Guns, things for guns, other weapons, things for other weapons, things that help you use and enhance the application of the stuff you get for your mind.

Any place and anything on this list has met three criteria: 1. I use them and/or refer to them now, or I have used them or referred to them in the past (that's one criteria with two parts) and consider them Good. 2. They come recommended by the people I respect and go to for knowledge and advice. 3. I believe they will offer you some kind of help or edge that you need or can use.

Don't expect me to be unbiased or 'fair' about my recommendations. Like you, I have limited resources to allocate to training and study, and I have no intention of pointing you at anything that I don't believe is worth every dollar and every minute that either of us have to allocate to something this important.

Let's get to the list now.

STUFF FOR YOUR MIND

Training resources:

For fight training:

Suarez International:
http://www.suarezinternationalstore.com/

  They will teach you how to prepare for the fight, how to conduct the fight, and how to get through the aftermath of the fight. They will teach you how to fight with more than just guns and they will teach you how to use more than just guns in the fight. They will not train you at the Lowest Common Denominator setting and they will not expect you to be stupid coming in. (Ignorant, yes, maybe, but not stupid. There is a difference between those two states that some schools and instructors don't appear to understand.) They will make you work, and they will make that work worth the effort you put into it. And you will be better at the end than you were at the beginning-- at <u>fighting</u>, not just at <u>shooting</u>.

  If you want to go to the gun-world equivalent of a dude ranch, if you want to be a gunfighter or an operator for a day or a weekend, there are other places to do that, and you are welcome to go to them.

  But if you want to become a gunfighter or a fighter, period-- if you want to learn what actual gunfighters and operators know and how to do it--go to Suarez International.

Sonny Puzikas: http://gospelofviolence.com/ and http://www.warriortalk.com/forumdisplay.php?175-Sonny-Puzikas-Training

  I have not taken a class from Sonny Puzikas. I have studied and learned from his DVD productions (and will continue to) and I have read what he has written (and will continue to). He is recommended by those that I listen to for advice about such things. Everything I have seen and everything I have heard of him and his instruction boils down to this: Invest in him, and he will give you things you need to win the fight with. 'Nuff said.

AMOK!: http://amokcombatives.com/

As with Sonny P's work, I have only so far been able to study work produced by Tom Sotis and his instructors. I have not been to an AMOK! class and have not received direct training. What I have seen and what I have heard of it to date, however, tells me this: If you want to learn about fighting with and against a knife, this is a very good place to go to do it.

Fight Focused Concepts: http://www.fightfocusedconcepts.com/

Roger Phillips is an excellent instructor who remains a keen student of the fight and who continues to develop that art and science of what it takes to win the fight. There is a reason I refer to and quote him as often as I do in this book.

Dynamic Response Training: http://dynamicresponsetraining.com/

Don Robinson worked in an Air Force special operations unit that was classified until six months before his retirement. His unit had to provide its own personnel and site security during many deployments. What he learned from that, and what he learned from others during and since that time, he is now passing on. I recommend you pay attention when he does that.

Dr. John Meade: http://www.statdoc.com/

Ignore the suit and tie photo. What's important to you is what he's doing in the second photo on that web page (he's the one in the background overseeing the drill): Teaching non-military-non-law-enforcement personnel (people like us, in other words) how to keep ourselves and others from dying even if we otherwise win the gunfight. He does that very well, too.

Study Resources: Stuff for your mind that's not training.

http://www.onesourcetactical.com/dvds.aspx

http://www.onesourcetactical.com/books.aspx

I find some things sometimes at websites like Amazon.com or Barnes and Noble, but that's mostly older material or historical reference. (I maintain a list of Medieval and Renaissance fighting system books that I want to get at Amazon, for example.) For the up-to-date material, One Source is where I look first. They have more than just SI-produced material there.

Other Web Resources: Sites and Forums

Warrior Talk web forum:
http://www.warriortalk.com

What? Do you think I would start anywhere else? That said, this web forum is <u>not</u> for everyone. For those it does fit, it can be very useful.

gospelofviolence.com

Sonny Puzika's web site.

Warrior Talk News

The SI newsletter and blog. Yes, there will be announcements and advertising of products and courses. There will also be articles and commentaries by SI instructors that you will find useful.

Paragon Pride web forum:
http://www.paragonpride.com/forum/

A recently (as of the time of this writing) started discussion forum with a growing list of very experienced and knowledgeable people in it, all ready to help you with questions and opinions about things you need to know.

www.guntoters.com

A small web site that is growing steadily. This one is going to be best suited to those just starting out with concealed carry and defensive use of the firearm.

www.inshadowinlight.com

My company website. I will be starting it up concurrent with the release of this book. It will begin by providing additional background about what is written here and additional information and support. Additional written and video work will be added on an ongoing basis there.

STUFF FOR YOUR HANDS

http://tsdcombatsystems.com/

The best guns and the best add-ons and accessories for those guns you can get. Period.

http://www.onesourcetactical.com/

Lots of other good stuff for your guns and for you.

http://www.cdnninvestments.com/

Pretty good source for magazines. You got pistols, you need magazines.

http://www.botach.com/

Good source of all kinds of gear for all kinds of things including guns.

ABOUT THE AUTHOR:

What <u>about</u> the author?

Lots of people can shoot better than I can. Lots of people can draw faster than I can. Lots of people can fight better than I can. Lots of people have more experience than I do.

Why aren't <u>they</u> writing a book like this, then?

Because for all the things they <u>can</u> do better, the one thing they <u>can't</u> do better, and the one thing that's most important to you that I <u>can</u> do better than a lot of people, is that I can teach better than they can.

I am a good student, I am a very good instructor, and I am an excellent communicator. Those are the most important things you need to know about me, because that's what makes it possible for me to do the job you need me to do here and on the range.

CR Williams

GRATITUDE

      The Lord, the God of Abraham, of Isaac, and of Jacob, and His son Jesus the Christ, the Risen One, have been both kinder and more merciful to me than I ever expected and certainly more than I deserve. He began equipping me to do this book and (what I hope to be) the ones to follow from the day I was born. He continues to develop me and equip me to best do the work He has for me to follow. I am grateful first to Him for that continuing mercy and those continuing blessings.

      One of the ways God set me up to do this was to bring me into close contact with Gabe Suarez, founder and CEO of the Suarez International group of companies. Both directly and indirectly, Gabe provided me with instruction and example of what to do and, as importantly, what not to do in regards to things like instructing others and in running a teaching business as a business. Without my exposure and interaction with both Gabe and the rest of the instructors on the Suarez International staff, I would have been inclined to stall out and occupy myself with self-pitying thoughts instead of starting another business that, among other things, produces the books in this series. I am grateful for that example and that exposure that kept me going.

The continuing support of what were once colleagues and now friends that I met while I was an SI Instructor have been an ongoing source of encouragement, so much so that I still sometimes slip and say "we" instead of "them" or "they" when speaking of SI and the people in it.

I would single out Rick Klopp, Jon Payne, and Tom Cornelius as particular examples of support and encouragement, and I thank them in particular and the SI Instructor Staff and their support personnel in general for the help I have received both inside and outside of the organization.

Some who were members of the SI instructor corps have, at the time of this writing, left the organization for various reasons. What remains is the help and support that provided me in the past and continue to provide me now. Roger Phillips, John Meade, Eric Pflieger and Chris Upchurch are of special note in that group.

I would be amiss if I did not express gratitude as well to those who had a hand in the actual production of this book: Photographer Lauvone Turner, Wilson Folmar, who loaned me the TSD pistol used in some of the photo sequences, and Craig DeLong, a friend who let me shove him around a bit when I needed to so I could make a point in a picture. I thank you, gentlemen, for your help with this project.

Finally, I must express gratitude to all the fighters and all the great teachers of the fight, whether with the gun or not, whether alive or not, whether they ever actually knew they were teaching me or not. In the end, what I do is to pass on what they in their stead passed on to me. In that respect, I stand on their shoulders even as I try to reach beyond them. If I am to honor their legacy and their contribution to the art and science of the fight, that's what I have to do. Gratitude, then, for what they have done and continue to do not just for me, but for everyone.

And thank **you**, whoever you are reading this, for purchasing this book and for giving me your consideration. I hope that you have received good compensation for the time and money you have invested here with me.

Now get back to training. See you in class. CR

Printed in Great Britain
by Amazon